Mollie MAKES

EMBROIDERY

15 NEW PROJECTS FOR YOU TO MAKE PLUS HANDY TECHNIQUES, TRICKS & TIPS

{Contents

Get stitching!

To get to my desk at Mollie Makes HQ, I walk past a wall of jewel-like embroidery threads each day. With its colour-coded, rainbow-bright satiny sheen, it's a little like treasure, and quite difficult to pass without wanting to reach out and gather up favourite colour combinations. I bet you feel the same way about your stash! So, we thought we'd bring together all our favourite stitchers in a range of impressive disciplines from cross stitch to crewel work to share their tips, stories and beautiful projects, inspiring us all to pick up a needle and thread.

Will you try Laura Trimmell's geometric squirrel (my favourite) or Nicole Vos Van Avezathe's quirky cloud-shaped pillow? Perhaps Clare Youngs' beautiful Folk Art throw (opposite) is more your thing? With seven different stitches to practise, it's one to stretch your skills for sure.

That's what we love about this collection – beginner or stitch-savvy, there really is something for everyone who fancies having a go. Need further encouragement? Flick to page 41. Michelle Galetta's Mama and baby owl ornaments are a must-stitch, simple as! There's a techniques section at the back to help you on your way. Hoops at the ready! Happy stitching.

Lara

Lara Watson
Editor, *Mollie Makes*

Projects

Working from patterns

{ There are two types of patterns used for the working of the embroidery projects in this book – the embroidery designs for stitching the surface embroidery motifs and the charted designs for working the counted thread techniques.

WORKING FROM CHARTED DESIGNS

To work the counted thread techniques featured, such as Bargello, counted cross stitch and canvaswork, a charted design must be followed. The stitches to be worked are indicated on a grid which represents the number of threads on the evenweave fabric you are working on. There are two types of chart – the solid box charts used for canvaswork and cross stitch, and the line chart used for the Bargello project.

Note

The trickiest thing about using a charted pattern is keeping your place. Depending on the size of the chart you may want to copy and enlarge it. Do not be afraid to write on your chart and use a highlighter to mark stopping points or completed sections.

SOLID BOX CHARTS

The charted pattern tells you where to place stitches and what colour and type of threads should be used, as identified in the colour key that runs alongside the chart. Each square on the chart represents one stitch. One cross stitch (counted cross stitch) is worked over two threads of evenweave fabric in each direction, or over one square of Aida fabric. One tent stitch (canvaswork) is worked over one strand of the canvas mesh.

LINE CHARTS

On the Bargello chart, the graph lines represent the fabric threads, and the exact position of each stitch is shown crossing the graph lines. Again, a key is provided to give the details of the thread colours used.

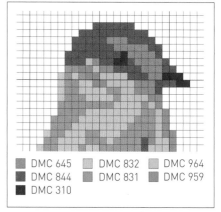

DMC 645   DMC 832   DMC 964
DMC 844   DMC 831   DMC 959
DMC 310

Example of solid box chart.

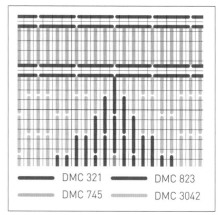

DMC 321   DMC 823
DMC 745   DMC 3042

Example of line chart.

WORKING FROM EMBROIDERY DESIGNS

The embroidery designs are your guide to stitching the outlines that will make up your project motif. They are reproduced as black-and-white line artworks to be as clear as possible to follow. Also, you will find that for many of the projects a thread colour and stitch diagram is supplied, to give you all the advice you'll need to replicate the stitched design.

Embroidery design.

THE EMBROIDERY DESIGN

The embroidery designs provided must be photocopied or traced and transferred onto your prepared fabric ready to begin stitching (see Getting Started, p. 88). It is not always possible to include these at the actual size used, and some may need to be enlarged using a photocopier or scanner. Where this is necessary the enlargement figure required is provided alongside the design.

It isn't always necessary to transfer every part of the embroidery design lines, and this is a case of personal preference. So for the decorative stitches on the polar bear's umbrella canopy on the cloud-shaped pillow (see p. 24), marking the position of the bullion rose with a dot may be all you need, and for the loop stitch, just a wavy line to keep your stitches even.

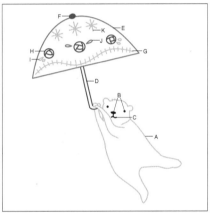

Thread colour and stitch diagram.

THE THREAD COLOUR AND STITCH DIAGRAM

For designs that feature lots of different colour threads and a variety of decorative stitches, the thread colour and stitch diagram provided will be your essential reference as you stitch. Each part of the design is annotated with letters (and sometimes numbers) that cross refer to a key to guide you to using the correct stitches, and to working with the right thread colours, using the number of thread strands required.

The colours used in the thread colour and stitch diagram are not always a perfect match of the thread colours used for the embroidery, and some colours may be exaggerated to differentiate between similar shades, or contrasted where the actual colour simply would not stand out on the page, as is often the case with white and cream for example.

Final stitching.

Mini glossary

Counted thread embroidery: Where stitches are accurately placed on evenweave or Aida fabric by counting the threads or squares.

Freestyle embroidery (aka surface embroidery): Embroidery worked by following a marked design or motif.

Outline stitches (aka line stitches): Stitches worked to define a motif.

Infill stitches (aka filling stitches): Stitches worked to fill a motif.

Simple stitch hoop pictures

These two woodland-themed pictures, framed for display in embroidery hoops, are perfect for a beginner as only one simple stitch is used – the humble backstitch. These embroideries are best completed wearing your cosiest sweater, with a cup of tea to hand.

MATERIALS

Two pieces of charcoal medium-weight linen, one piece 25cm (10in) square and one piece 20.5cm (8in) square

Stranded cotton (floss): dark yellow (DMC 725), red (DMC 321)

Embroidery needle size 5

Wooden embroidery hoops: 18cm (7in) diameter and 13cm (5in) diameter

Hot glue gun

SIZE

Cabin in the woods: 18cm (7in) diameter
Squirrel: 13cm (5in) diameter

STITCHES

Backstitch (p. 92)

FEATURED TECHNIQUES

- Preparing fabric and threads (p. 89)
- Using a hoop (p. 88)
- Transferring designs (p. 88)

LAURA TRIMMELL

Laura Trimmell, creator of CuriousDoodles, fell in love with the tactile quality of embroidery while studying graphic design. CuriousDoodles embroidery kits add pattern, geometry and unusual materials to a very traditional craft. Her modern kits are available at CuriousDoodles.com.

Embroidery Story

Embroidery is how I relax my mind and force myself to slow down. I find it's the little things that help a project go smoother – for example, I prepare several needles with thread before I start stitching, so I don't have to stop to rethread. Keep all of your project materials in a clear zip-lock bag so nothing gets lost, and it's easy to throw in your handbag for stitching on the go.

METHOD

{01} Prepare your fabric

As these designs are intended to be displayed as wall art, there is no need to prewash the fabric, but do give it a good press with a steam iron. Then cut your fabric down so that you have at least 5–7.5cm (2–3in) clearance all the way around the finished size of the design.

{02} Transfer the embroidery design

If using a darker fabric like the one featured, transfer the squirrel design to the smaller piece of fabric and the cabin in the woods design to the larger piece of fabric using the pricking method (see p. 88). If you choose to work on a light fabric, the light-box method works best.

{03} Embroider the cabin in the woods design

Place the larger piece of fabric in the 18cm (7in) diameter embroidery hoop. Using three strands of red thread in the needle, start by stitching the silhouette of the house using backstitch, before working the trees with the yellow thread. When embroidering the trees, start in one corner and work your way across the design. To work the complete design, which is designed to extend beyond the edge of the hoop frame when displayed as a picture, it will be necessary to reposition the fabric in the hoop; centre the area you are working on in the hoop.

{04} Embroider the squirrel design

Place the smaller piece of fabric in the 13cm (5in) diameter embroidery hoop. Using three strands of red thread in the needle, start at the edge of the squirrel in the face area and work backstitch to connect the dots one small section at a time, making sure to complete all the stitches before moving on to the next section, working your way down the squirrel's arm and body to finish in the tail area. Mostly, you will be able to connect the dots with only one stitch, but if you have to cover a distance wider than the nail on your pinky finger, you should divide it into two or even three stitches, as large stitches on the front (or the back) of the fabric can result in unsightly stretching. Check your stitching and fill in any missing stitches.

{05} Prepare the hoops for hanging

Remove the embroideries from the hoops and press. Secure the pressed embroideries back in their respective hoops, making sure to centre the designs as you wish taking care not to overstretch the fabric. (Remember, the cabin in the woods design is supposed to go past the edge of the hoop.) Trim the excess fabric all the way around the back rim of the hoops to approx 1cm (⅜in). Still working on the reverse, use the hot glue gun to apply a 7.5cm (3in) length of glue on the inside hoop. Tuck and press the trimmed fabric allowance into the glue to secure it before moving on to the next section. Take your time to work incrementally around the hoop. Let the glue dry completely before hanging your hoop pictures.

When stitching the squirrel design you often have to insert your needle into a hole that already has stitches in it. Use the needle tip to push existing stitches aside to go directly into the hole as putting thread through thread will make it bunch up and catch.

EMBROIDERY DESIGNS

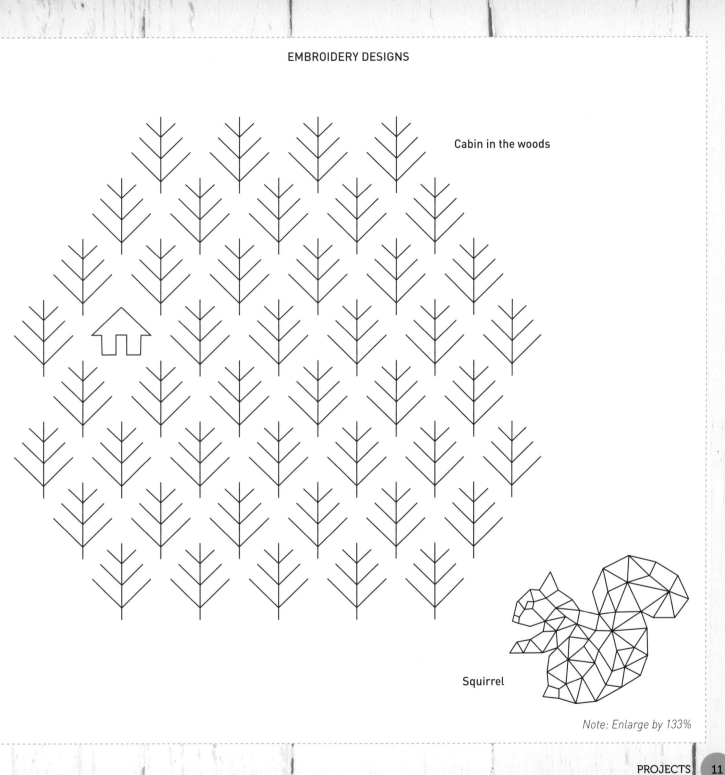

Cabin in the woods

Squirrel

Note: Enlarge by 133%

In the frame greetings cards

Have fun playing with the ten basic embroidery stitches and make something truly personal for your loved ones with this lovely collection of six designs. Each card features an adorably cute critter with a little space to add the initials or name of the recipient. These designs are great for any occasion, from a baby shower to a birthday.

MATERIALS

One piece of cream muslin or quilting-weight cotton 30.5cm (12in) square for each greetings card

Stranded cotton (floss): light green (DMC 704), yellow (DMC 973), golden brown (DMC 3826), white (DMC B5200), blue (DMC 3843), pink (DMC 605), orange (DMC 946), yellow-orange (DMC 741), black (DMC 310), grey (DMC 415), purple (DMC 553)

Embroidery needle size 5

Embroidery hoop 15–20.5cm (6–8in) diameter

Heavy craft paper or scrapbook cardstock in the colour of your choice

Pinking shears, cutting mat, metal ruler, craft knife, bone folder and fabric-basting spray adhesive

SIZE

Finished card: 12.5 x 18cm (5 x 7in)

STITCHES

Backstitch (p. 92)
Running stitch (p. 93)
Cross stitch (p. 94)
Herringbone stitch (p. 95)
Stem stitch (p. 96)
Chain stitch (p. 97)
Blanket stitch (p. 98)
Satin stitch (p. 99)
French knot (p. 100)
Feather stitch (p. 101)

FEATURED TECHNIQUES

• Preparing fabric and threads (p. 89)
• Using a hoop (p. 88)
• Transferring designs (p. 88)

ALYSSA THOMAS

Alyssa Thomas is the owner and designer of Penguin & Fish, a manufacturer of lovely and quirky hand embroidery patterns, kits, sewing patterns and artful plush. Alyssa is also the author of the craft book *Sew & Stitch Embroidery* and a fabric designer for Clothworks Textiles. She's on her way to the dream of drawing animals all day long. Check out penguinandfish.com and facebook.com/penguinandfish for more information.

METHOD

{01} Prepare your fabric and threads

Using a pencil or water-soluble marker, draw an 11.5cm (4½in) square in the centre of your piece of fabric. You may find it useful to use a thread organiser (see p. 87) to sort the stranded cottons you will require to stitch your chosen design.

{02} Transfer the embroidery design

Using either the light-box or the carbon transfer paper method, transfer the embroidery design of your choice onto the fabric, centring it in the marked square. To personalise the card, write a name (or initials) in the centre of the design. You can either do this freehand or use the font provided, reducing or enlarging it to fit.

{03} Embroider the design

Place your prepared fabric in the embroidery hoop. Using three strands of thread in the needle, stitch the embroidery using the thread colour and stitch diagram for your chosen design. The order of stitching is a case of personal preference but the following is recommended:

Bird card: Branch, bird's beak and yellow-orange berries, body outline and blue berries, bird's eye.

Fish card: Light green seaweed, blue seaweed, yellow fin lines on fish tail, fish outline, mouth and eyes.

Mouse card: Yellow-orange, then yellow cheese parts, mouse tail, ears and nose, body outline, eyes.

Note

For the mouse card the cheese is stitched before the main outline of the mouse as that way the backstitch outline of the mouse's paw will cover up the satin stitch start and finish points, to give the impression that the mouse's paw is in front of the cheese. Stitch all of one colour thread before moving on to the next – this helps to keep your workspace uncluttered, and it will give you a wonderful sense of accomplishment.

Elephant card: Elephant's ears and tail, body outline, top water spray, middle water spray, bottom water spray, eyes.

Lamb card: Fence, black outlines of lamb and eye, nose, fleece.

Beaver card: Beaver's teeth, tail cross stitches, tail outline, remaining outline starting with the legs and ears, nose, grey log, black log, eyes.

Remove the embroidered fabric from the hoop and press carefully. Using the pinking shears, cut out the embroidery along the marked 11.5cm (4½in) square guideline. Use a damp cloth to remove any remaining water-soluble marker from the embroidery, then set aside to dry.

{04} Make the card

Working on a cutting mat, use a metal ruler and craft knife to cut a 25 x 18cm (10 x 7in) rectangle from the card. Alternatively, use a pencil to lightly draw the rectangle onto the card, then carefully cut out with a pair of scissors.

Working on the inside of the card, use the ruler and bone folder to score a line down the middle of the card rectangle so that when it is folded it makes a 12.5 x 18cm (5 x 7in) card.

THREAD COLOUR AND STITCH DIAGRAMS

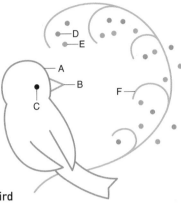

Bird

Note: 3 strands of DMC stranded cotton (floss) used
A blue (3843) backstitch
B yellow-orange (741) backstitch
C black (310) French knot
D blue (3843) French knot
E yellow-orange (741) French knot
F light green (704) stem stitch

Mouse

Note: 3 strands of DMC stranded cotton (floss) used
A yellow (973) satin stitch
B yellow-orange (741) satin stitch
C pink (605) chain stitch
D purple (553) backstitch
E black (310) French knot
F pink (605) satin stitch

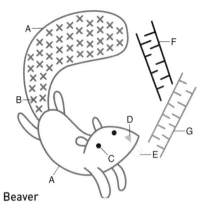

Beaver

Note: 3 strands of DMC stranded cotton (floss) used
A golden brown (3826) backstitch
B golden brown (3826) cross stitch
C black (310) French knot
D pink (605) satin stitch
E yellow (973) backstitch
F black (310) blanket stitch
G grey (415) blanket stitch

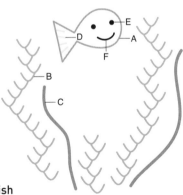

Fish

Note: 3 strands of DMC stranded cotton (floss) used
A yellow-orange (741) backstitch
B light green (704) feather stitch
C blue (3843) chain stitch
D yellow (973) backstitch
E black (310) French knot
F black (310) backstitch

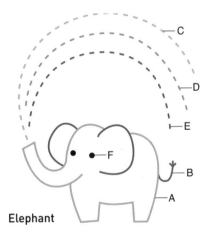

Elephant

Note: 3 strands of DMC stranded cotton (floss) used
A yellow-orange (741) backstitch
B orange (946) backstitch
C light green (704) running stitch
D blue (3843) running stitch
E purple (553) running stitch
F black (310) French knot

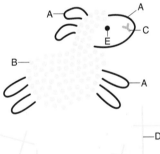

Lamb

Note: 3 strands of DMC stranded cotton (floss) used
A black (310) backstitch
B white (B5200) French knot
C pink (605) backstitch
D yellow (973) herringbone stitch
E black (310) French knot

{05} Attach the fabric to the card
Lay the embroidered fabric wrong side up on a paper towel, and lightly spray with the fabric-basting spray adhesive, following the manufacturer's instructions.

Take the folded card and open it out onto a flat surface so that the back of the card is on the left and the front of the card is on the right. Carefully position the embroidered fabric square 1cm (⅜in) from the top edge so that it is centred horizontally on the front of the card.

Using a sewing thread shade to match the colour of the card, machine stitch 6mm (¼in) from the edge of the fabric square. Alternatively, hand stitch the border with running stitch.

{06} Embroider onto the card
To add a little more texture to your finished greeting card, you can embroider a few stitches onto the card itself. Add a cluster of French knots, a running stitch line, or even a simple greeting.

First use a pencil to lightly draw your design onto the card. Pierce a hole at the starting point and begin your embroidery, leaving a 12.5cm (5in) thread tail. Lightly tape or hold the thread end out of the way as you embroider the design details onto the card, pre-punching the holes with the needle as you go. When complete, weave the thread ends into the back of the stitches on the inside of the card, then trim. Erase any pencil marks from the front of the card.

Embroidery Story

At Penguin & Fish we love stitching anything with little animals on it and the opportunity embroidery gives us to easily personalise a project. The greetings card collection combines these two things beautifully, while showcasing fun ways to use basic embroidery stitches – my favourite is using the feather stitch for seaweed in the fish design. Instead of greetings cards, you could turn your embroideries into Christmas tree ornaments by sewing them onto felt, or combine them with fabric squares for a simple baby quilt.

EMBROIDERY DESIGNS

Bird

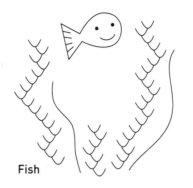

Fish

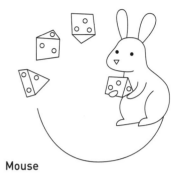

Mouse

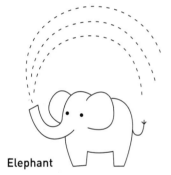

Elephant

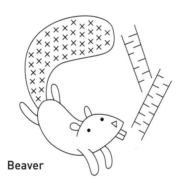

Beaver

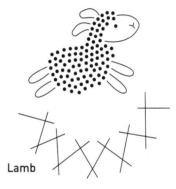

Lamb

A B C D E F G H I J K
L M N O P Q R S T
U V W X Y Z

a b c d e f g h i j k l m
n o p q r s t u v w x y z
0 1 2 3 4 5 6 7 8 9

Alphabet

Note: Enlarge by 200%

Russian dolls wall hanging

Bring a touch of folk art into your home with this super bright wall hanging, decorated with the ever-popular matryoshka motif. These Russian nesting dolls offer endless possibilities for pattern and colour. While each is outlined in backstitch, the infill stitches have been varied, and you can easily use different stitches if you choose to.

MATERIALS

One piece of white quilting-weight cotton approx 35 x 30cm (13¾ x 11¾in)

Stranded cotton (floss): yellow (DMC 307), egg yolk yellow (DMC 972), bright yellow (DMC 973), orange (DMC 741), dark orange (DMC 606), red (DMC 666), pale pink (DMC 894), light pink (DMC 957), pink (DMC 956), dark pink (DMC 602), magenta (DMC 917), green (DMC 907), light green (DMC 3819), sea green (DMC 3851), turquoise (DMC 3846), light blue (DMC 996), blue (DMC 3843), black (DMC 310)

Embroidery needle size 7

Embroidery hoop 25cm (10in) diameter

One piece of floral print quilting cotton approx 30cm (11¾in) square for the front

One piece of dark pink quilting cotton approx 30cm (11¾in) square for the back

80 x 40cm (31½ x 15¾in) lightweight interfacing

45cm (17¾in) length of red mini pom-pom fringe

Matching sewing thread

SIZE

Finished hanging: approx 26 x 26.5cm (10¼ x 10½in)

STITCHES

Backstitch (p. 92)
Cross stitch (p. 94)
Satin stitch (p. 99)
French knot (p. 100)
Arrowhead stitch (p. 104)
St George's cross stitch (p. 111)
Ermine stitch (p. 114)
Leaf stitch (p. 114)
Scroll stitch (p. 119)
Fly stitch (p. 123)
Zigzag chain stitch (p. 124)
Petal stitch (p. 129)
Cloud filling stitch (p. 137)

FEATURED TECHNIQUES
• Preparing fabric and threads (p. 89)
• Using a hoop (p. 88)
• Transferring designs (p. 88)

METHOD

{01} Transfer the embroidery design

Using the light-box method and a water-soluble marker, transfer the embroidery design to the prepared white quilting cotton fabric.

{02} Embroider the design

Place the fabric in an embroidery hoop, if you choose to use one. Using three strands of thread in the needle, stitch the embroidery using the thread colour and stitch diagram as your guide. Start by stitching the outlines of the dress, scarf, face and apron for each of the dolls. Then work the filling stitches on the aprons and scarves, and embroider the patterns on the dresses. Embroider the facial details – eyes, nose, cheeks, mouth – using just two strands of thread in the needle.

To embroider the border, use three strands of thread in the needle and first stitch the leaves in the corners, then finish off with the zigzag chain stitch along each border edge.

Remove the embroidered fabric from the hoop and rinse off the pattern drawing. Once the fabric is dry, gently press it (see note on p. 89). Cut the fabric to size, trimming it to 22.5 x 17.5cm (8⅞ x 6⅞ in).

THREAD COLOUR AND STITCH DIAGRAM

Note: 3 strands of DMC stranded cotton (floss) used unless specified otherwise
A light green (3819) zigzag chain stitch
B light green (3819) leaf stitch
C red (666) backstitch
D dark orange (606) fly stitch
E orange (741) French knot
F light blue (996) backstitch
G light blue (996) petal stitch
H yellow (307) ermine stitch
I pink (956) backstitch
J magenta (917) and green (907) cloud filling stitch
K turquoise (3846) backstitch

L turquoise (3846) petal stitch
M egg yolk yellow (972) St George's cross stitch
N dark pink (602) backstitch
O sea green (3851) and green (907) arrowhead stitch
P blue (3843) backstitch
Q blue (3843) petal stitch
R bright yellow (973) cross stitch
S light pink (957) backstitch
T pink (956) and green (907) scroll stitch
U red (666) satin stitch – 2 strands
V pale pink (894) satin stitch – 2 strands
W black (310) satin stitch – 2 strands

Embroidery Story

I never did any embroidery until about six or seven years ago, but it was love at first stitch. Now a day doesn't feel quite right if I haven't done at least a bit of embroidery. Thread, pretty colours, pattern – what's not to love! Russian dolls are traditionally decorated with flowers, but I think they are perfect for trying out new stitches. Once you've made the wall hanging, you could stitch a doll or two on cushion covers to match, because, in my opinion, you can never have too many Russian dolls!

CARINA ENVOLDSEN-HARRIS

Carina Envoldsen-Harris is a designer, blogger and author. Originally from Denmark, she now lives just outside London with her English husband. Painting, drawing, ceramics – Carina has always made things. Under the name Polka & Bloom she creates colourful embroidery patterns and fabric designs. To see more of her work visit her blog: carinascraftblog.com.

{03} Cut and prepare fabrics

From the printed cotton (front fabric), cut one piece measuring 27.5 x 5cm (10¾ x 2in), two pieces measuring 17.5 x 5cm (6⅞ x 2in), and one piece measuring 27.5 x 9cm (10¾ x 3½in).

From the dark pink cotton (backing fabric), cut one piece measuring 27.5 x 20.5cm (10¾ x 8in) and one piece measuring 27.5 x 9cm (10¾ x 3½in).

Iron interfacing to the wrong side of all the pieces of fabric (front, back and embroidered). Take the dark pink and printed cotton strips measuring 27.5 x 9cm (10¾ x 3½in) and use the scallop-edged template on p. 156 to cut a scallop along one long edge of each of the strips.

{04} Make wall hanging front

Note: Use a 1cm (⅜in) seam allowance.

With right sides facing, sew the short printed cotton strips to the short sides of the embroidered panel. Press the seams towards the outer edge. With right sides facing, sew the long strip of printed cotton to the top edge of the embroidered panel. Press the seams towards the outer edge. Finally, take the printed cotton scallop-edged strip and align the straight edge to the bottom edge of the embroidered piece with right sides facing, and sew in place. Press the seams towards the outer edge as before.

{05} Make wall hanging back

Note: Use a 1cm (⅜in) seam allowance.

Pin the straight edge of the pink cotton scallop-edged strip to the large pink cotton back piece, with right sides facing. Make a mark approx 6cm (2⅜in) from both sides along the pinned edge. Sew from the edge to each mark, to leave a generous turning gap in the middle.

{06} Assemble the wall hanging

Pin the front and back pieces together, with right sides facing. At the top edge, make a mark 2cm (¾in) in from each side. Using these marks as your guide, pin the ends of the pom-pom fringe in place between the two layers of fabric. If the pom-pom fringe is a bit bulky at the seam, cut off one or two pom-poms.

Sew the front and back pieces together with a 6mm (¼in) seam allowance. Where the scallops meet, do not sew a point; pivot the work when your needle is approx 1cm (⅜in) below the point, sew two or three stitches parallel to the point, then pivot the work back and continue to follow the curve on the next scallop.

Clip the corners and cut around the curves with pinking shears (or snip little triangles along the curves using a small pair of scissors). At the points where the scallops meet, it is important to cut away as much fabric as you can, but take care not to snip into the seam. Also, make a tiny snip in each of the corners between the curved seam and the stitches that are parallel with the point, as this will help to make the scallop points as smooth as possible.

Turn the hanging through to the right side, carefully pushing out the corners and the scallops. If points between scallops are not lying flat, remove a little more fabric. Slip stitch the opening closed and press the wall hanging to finish.

When sewing the scallop edge, mark the seam allowance to ensure you get the curve as smooth as possible. Work slowly – stop and pivot the work under the needle every few stitches. This will take more time, but the end result will be so much the better for it.

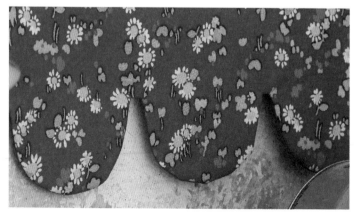

Seam allowance

EMBROIDERY DESIGN

Note: Enlarge by 133%

Cloud-shaped pillow

What could be better for a daytime nap than this cloud-shaped pillow, embroidered with a sweet kitty and a perky polar bear, scuttling across a windy sky, hanging off their umbrella handles as they dodge the raindrops. Each umbrella canopy is filled with lines of decorative stitches, serving as mini stitch samplers.

MATERIALS

One piece of white cotton fabric approx 63.5 x 45.5cm (25 x 18in)

Stranded cotton (floss): grey (DMC 169), very dark grey (DMC 3799), dark orange (DMC 3853), light turquoise (DMC 598), pink (DMC 761), light brown (DMC 434), tan brown (DMC 436), light hazelnut brown (DMC 422), dark turquoise (DMC 3810), olive green (DMC 834), dark green (DMC 580), lime green (DMC 166), red (DMC 321), white (DMC blanc)

Needles: crewel sizes 3–8 depending on your preference; milliner's (or straw) needle size 3 or 5

Embroidery frame/hoop: 28cm (11in) square Q-Snap frame and 13cm (5in) diameter hoop

One piece of printed fabric approx 63.5 x 45.5cm (25 x 18in) for the backing

Wadding approx 63.5 x 45.5cm (25 x 18in)

Polyester filling

All-purpose sewing thread

SIZE

Finished pillow: 54.5 x 32.5cm (21¼ x 12¾in)

STITCHES

Backstitch (p. 92)
Stem stitch (p. 96)
Detached chain stitch (p. 97)
Satin stitch (p. 99)

Straight stitch (p. 102)
Split stitch (p. 103)
Arrowhead stitch (p. 104)
Star filling stitch (p. 112)
Ermine stitch (p. 114)
Bullion stitch roses (p. 117)
Knotted buttonhole stitch (p. 120)
Loop stitch (p. 122)
Zigzag chain stitch (p. 124)
Wheatear stitch (p. 127)
Whipped running stitch (p. 132)

FEATURED TECHNIQUES

- Frames (p. 87)
- Using a hoop (p. 88)
- Transferring designs (p. 88)

METHOD

{01} Prepare your fabric

Using the pillow template (p. 157), mark the outline of the cloud on the white cotton fabric with a water-soluble marker. Trace the cat and polar bear embroidery designs onto two separate pieces of tracing paper, and decide where you want to place them on the white cotton fabric, making sure to position them at least 2.5cm (1in) from the inner edge of the cloud marking. Once you have found the perfect position, mark the placing of the umbrella button with a light pencil mark.

{02} Transfer embroidery designs

Using the light-box method, transfer the cat and polar bear designs to the white cotton fabric, remembering to align the umbrella buttons with the marks you made in step 1.
(Note: The raindrops will be marked onto the fabric after the cat and polar bear designs have been embroidered.)

{03} Embroider the cat design

Place the fabric so that the cat design is centred in the large square embroidery frame, and begin the embroidery, working the design in the following order, using the thread colour and stitch diagram as your guide.
(Note: Four strands of embroidery thread are used unless otherwise specified.)

Outline of cat: Start by stitching the grey split stitch outline, and use a few backstitches to create the angular shape at either side of the head. Stitch the paws and tail tip to complete the cat's outline.

Facial features: Work small satin stitch eyes and a backstitch mouth

---

THREAD COLOUR AND STITCH DIAGRAM

Note: 4 strands of DMC stranded cotton (floss) used unless specified otherwise

A grey (169) split stitch
B white (blanc) split stitch
C very dark grey (3799) satin stitch – 1 strand
D very dark grey (3799) backstitch – 1 strand
E pink (761) satin stitch – 2 strands
F white (blanc) straight stitch – 2 strands
G white (blanc) backstitch – 1 strand
H tan brown (436) stem stitch
I dark turquoise (3810) backstitch – 3 strands
J dark turquoise (3810) knotted buttonhole stitch
   – 3 strands
K red (321) satin stitch – 2 strands
L olive green (834) zigzag chain stitch
   – 3 strands
M whipped running stitch using light turquoise (598)
   for the running stitch and dark turquoise (3810)
   for the whipping stitch
N dark orange (3853) wheatear stitch
O light turquoise (598) ermine stitch – 3 strands
P lime green (166) arrowhead stitch – 3 strands

using one strand of thread. Use two strands for the nose. Work whiskers using one long straight stitch with two strands of thread, and the ear 'fluff' with two backstitches each using one strand of thread.

Outline of umbrella: Stitch the handle first; then embroider the curved backstitch canopy with three strands of thread; and the knotted buttonhole stitch base with three strands of thread, this time using your milliner's needle. Embroider the button at the top of the canopy with two strands of thread.

Decorative infill on umbrella: Choose to work the decorative bands of infill stitches either from the top or from the bottom as you prefer.

Detail of cat embroidery.

{04} Embroider the polar bear design

Place the fabric so that the polar bear design is centred in the small embroidery hoop, and begin the embroidery, working the design in the following order, using the thread colour and stitch diagram as your guide.

(Note: Three strands of embroidery thread are used unless otherwise specified.)

Outline of polar bear: Use four strands of embroidery thread and backstitch, but keep the stitches small in the detailed areas such as the ears.

Facial features: Using only one strand of thread, work tiny satin stitches for the eyes and nose, and backstitches for the mouth.

Outline of umbrella: Stitch the handle first, then the canopy. Embroider the button at the top of the canopy with two strands of thread.

Decorative infill on umbrella: Choose to work the decorative bands of infill stitches either from the top or from the bottom as you prefer.

THREAD COLOUR AND STITCH DIAGRAM

Note: 3 strands of DMC stranded cotton (floss) used unless specified otherwise

A light hazelnut brown (422) backstitch – 4 strands
B very dark grey (3799) satin stitch – 1 strand
C very dark grey (3799) backstitch – 1 strand
D light brown (434) stem stitch
E dark orange (3853) stem stitch
F dark turquoise (3810) satin stitch – 2 strands
G light turquoise (598) loop stitch
H red (321) bullion stitch roses
I lime green (166) detached chain stitch – 2 strands
J dark green (580) detached chain stitch – 2 strands
K olive green (834) star filling stitch

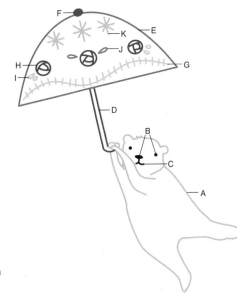

{05} Mark and embroider the raindrops

Use a water-soluble pen to mark small slanted strokes about 6mm (¼in) long spread evenly across the cloud, making sure to position them at least 2.5cm (1in) from the inner edge. Stitch the raindrops freehand using satin stitch and two strands of thread from a selection of thread colours used for the infill bands on the umbrella canopies. Start with one long stitch in the middle and add smaller stitches to either side to fill up the drop-shape.

{06} Prepare the pillow fabrics

Give the embroidered fabric a gentle hand wash, rinse well and leave it to line-dry. When it is nearly dry, carefully press the embroidery from the back. Use the cloud template to re-draw the outline of the cloud onto the embroidered fabric, double checking that you have the placement of the embroidered characters correct before lightly marking a dotted line around the template with either an air-soluble pen or a soft pencil. Cut the cloud shape out on the marked line.

Pin the cloud template to the wadding and cut out. Unpin the template from the wadding, then cut off another 1.3cm (½in) all the way around the wadding and set aside.

Finally use the cloud template to cut out the pillow backing from the wrong side of the patterned fabric.

Place the embroidered cloud onto the cloud backing with right sides facing. Mark the centre point of the base of the cloud with a pin, then measure 10cm (4in) to the left (or right) and mark with a pin again – this gap will be used to fill your pillow later. Pin all the way around the edge of the cloud, leaving the turning gap unpinned.

{07} Sew and stuff the pillow

Machine stitch around the pinned edge of the cloud using a 1.3cm (½in) seam allowance. Cut triangle shapes from the seam allowance on the curved areas, taking care not to cut into the seam; then trim the seam allowance to 6mm (¼in). Turn the pillow cover the right way out and press carefully on the back only.

Turn the cover back through to the wrong side with the back of the embroidered side facing you. Place the wadding on top of the cover – it should be a tiny bit smaller than the seam line, and you should trim to adjust slightly if necessary. A light press should make the wadding stick to the fabric to keep it in place, but do check the manufacturer's instructions first.

Turn the pillow inside out very carefully, and if necessary adjust the placing of the wadding. Stuff the pillow using little bits of stuffing at a time to avoid lumpiness. Once you are happy with the feel of your pillow, close the gap with ladder stitch.

Embroidery Story

I call my design 'Happy when it rains', and it is inspired by Mary Poppins and the great British weather! It combines my love for stitching cute critters with my passion for stitch samplers, and the umbrella canopies are stuffed with decorative stitch borders.

NICOLE VOS VAN AVEZATHE

Nicole Vos van Avezathe (aka Follow the White Bunny) makes embroidery and craft patterns that are often sweet, sometimes odd and always original. Her designs include sea-faring hedgehogs in a tea-cup boat, and a storybook favourite, the princess and the pea. An avid stitcher, Nicole likes to encourage embroiderers to try new techniques – followthewhitebunny.com.

EMBROIDERY DESIGNS

Cat

Polar bear

Note: Enlarge by 133%

Folk art throw

The folk art embroidery of Scandinavia and Eastern Europe inspired this design for a lovely linen throw with colourful stitched borders. It evokes the patterns and motifs of traditional embroidery, yet it has a fresh, contemporary look – and its scalloped stitched edge makes an edging trim completely unnecessary.

MATERIALS

One piece of linen fabric 82 x 102cm (32¼ x 40in)

Stranded cotton (floss): three skeins each of dark orange (DMC 720), pink (DMC 600), mid green (DMC 470), blue (DMC 322), olive green (DMC 834); four skeins of pale blue (DMC 597)

Darner needle size 1–5

One piece of gingham fabric 82 x 102cm (32¼ x 40in) for backing

SIZE

Finished throw: 80 x 100cm (31½ x 39¼in)

STITCHES

Backstitch (p. 92)
Running stitch (p. 93)
Straight stitch (p. 102)
Seed stitch (p. 105)
Bullion stitch (p. 117)
Double knot stitch (p. 118)
Threaded backstitch (p. 134)

FEATURED TECHNIQUES

- Transferring designs (p. 88)

CLARE YOUNGS

After working as a graphic designer and illustrator for a number of years, Clare turned to craft full time five years ago and she has not looked back since. She spends her day doing what she loves best – snipping, sewing, designing and making things. Catch up with her crafty way of life on her blog at clareyoungs.co.uk.

METHOD

{01} Transfer the embroidery design

Enlarge the embroidery design and use the light-box method to transfer it along the full width at either end of the linen fabric: place the design tracing 3cm (1⅛in) down from the fabric edge and start at the top right side; then flip the tracing over to complete the top left side, aligning the tracing over the three diamond shapes on the central motif.

{02} Embroider the design

The embroidery is worked with all six strands of thread in the needle, and a hoop or frame is not required. Use the thread colour and stitch diagram as your guide. The design is made up of seven motifs across the border and a line of scalloped stitching along the edge, and it can be very satisfying to complete one motif at a time, moving along

the throw, and then finish with the scalloped edging.

Most of the bullion stitches are worked to approx 6mm (¼in) with the thread wound around the needle five times except as follows.

Edge of central motif: Start with a small bullion stitch at the top of each side, winding the thread three times around the needle, increasing by one wind each bullion stitch until

---

THREAD COLOUR AND STITCH DIAGRAM

Note: 6 strands of DMC stranded cotton (floss) used

Stitches
A threaded backstitch
B backstitch
C double knot stitch
D straight stitch
E bullion stitch (see step 2 for details)
F seed stitch

Thread colours
—— blue (322)
—— dark orange (720)
—— pink (600)
—— pale blue (597)
—— olive green (834)
—— mid green (470)

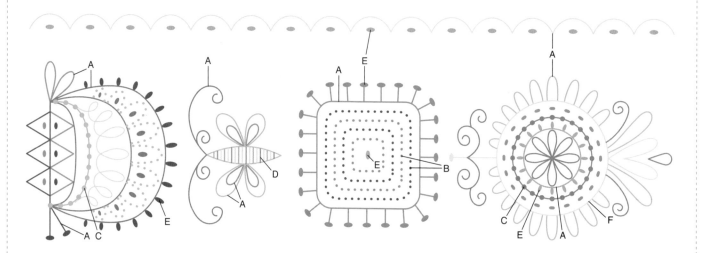

eight winds. Stitch five knots with eight winds, then decrease in size as you go around to work the last knot with two winds.

Centre of square motif: Eight winds.
Inner circle of end motifs: Work with four winds.

{03} Make the throw

Place the front and backing fabrics right sides together and pin all around the edge. Sew together with a 1cm (⅜in) seam allowance, leaving a turning gap of approx 18cm (7in). Trim corners, turn right way out and slip stitch the gap closed.

{04} Embroider the running stitch lines

The throw has three lines of evenly stitched running stitches in colours

Embroidery Story

Until five years ago, my only experience of embroidery was stitching the obligatory needle case onto Binca as a very young child at school. Now I'm hooked – it's very satisfying to hold a finished piece of embroidery in your hands, knowing that you have worked every stitch. I love how portable embroidery is – you can carry it around in your bag and stitch anywhere. Some of this throw was embroidered sitting under the shade of a fig tree in Spain, and another section while waiting for a dentist's appointment!

chosen from the motif designs. To place the first line of stitching, fold the throw in half and press along the crease. Use the pressed line as a guide to sew running stitches across the width of the throw through both layers of fabric.

To place the second line of stitching, fold in the throw from one side, lining up the edge with the first row of running stitches, and press to give you a guideline. Sew a line of running stitch along this guideline using a different colour thread. Repeat at the other end of the throw to stitch the third row of running stitch. Press the throw to finish.

EMBROIDERY DESIGN

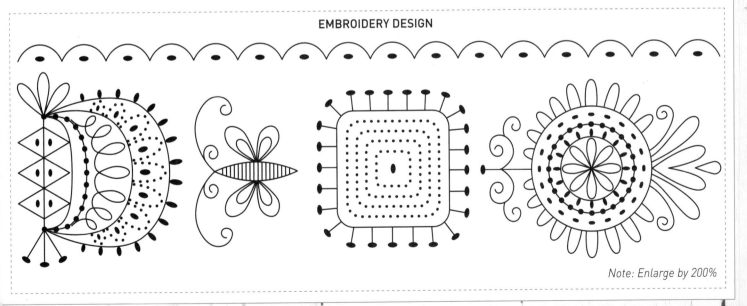

Note: Enlarge by 200%

Pretty posy ribbon runner

Using gorgeous ribbons on a simple linen background, this charming floral runner will brighten your table like a freshly cut bouquet. Learning the stitches is deceptively easy and you'll soon find that you've stitched up an impressive display.

MATERIALS

0.5m (½yd) of 112cm (44in) wide linen fabric

4mm wide 100% River Silks silk embroidery ribbon: one spool each of purple (204), golden yellow (250), dark green (235); two spools of orange (156)

7mm wide 100% River Silks silk embroidery ribbon: one spool each of bright green (130), yellow (97)

Stranded cotton (floss): dark purple (DMC 333), dark green (DMC 904), black (DMC 310)

Needles: chenille size 18; embroidery size 5

Embroidery hoops: 25cm (10in) and 13cm (5in) diameter

112cm (44in) wide quilting cotton: 15cm (6in) yellow print for end panels; 1.5m (1½yd) purple solid for backing

SIZE

Finished runner: 135 x 43cm (53 x 17in)

STITCHES

Stem stitch (p. 96)
Lazy daisy (see detached chain stitch, p. 97)
French knot (p. 100)
Straight stitch (p. 102)
Coral stitch (p. 116)
Bullion stitch (p. 117)
Ribbon stitch (p. 141)
Spider web rose (p. 142)

FEATURED TECHNIQUES

- Using a hoop (p. 88)
- Transferring designs (p. 88)
- Silk ribbon embroidery (p. 139)

(MOLLIE JOHANSON)

Mollie Johanson is most comfortable with some stitching in hand. She began her blog Wild Olive as a creative outlet, and her dreaming and doodling have resulted in numerous embroidery and paper projects, most featuring simply expressive faces. Mollie lives near Chicago, commuting daily to her in-home studio via the coffee pot. Learn more at molliejohanson.com.

METHOD

{01} Prepare your fabric and threads
Prewash and iron your fabrics. Soak your ribbon in cold, salted water to rinse away extra dye and set the colour. Cut the linen fabric to 46 x 112cm (18⅛ x 44in).

{02} Transfer the embroidery design
Using the light-box method and an air-soluble pen, trace the posy design in the centre of the linen fabric and the corner motif 5cm (2in) in from each corner (see p. 38 for embroidery designs). When tracing, it's not necessary to transfer the details of the stitches in the design; just trace the basic shape of each stitch, then refer to the ribbon and thread colour and stitch diagram as you work. Use a tea plate (approx 21cm/8¼in diameter) to mark a circle to contain the posy motif.

{03} Embroider the central flower
Cut a piece of 7mm wide yellow ribbon and lock it onto your chenille needle (p. 140). Working in an embroidery hoop, start by stitching the straight stitches that form the petals of the large central flower. For the circle of French knots, use 4mm wide orange ribbon and stitch them right next to each other, working as many as are required to form a solid

RIBBON AND THREAD COLOUR AND STITCH DIAGRAM

Note: River Silks and DMC stranded cotton (floss) have been used

4mm ribbon colours
- purple (204)
- orange (156)
- golden yellow (250)
- dark green (235)

7mm ribbon colours
- bright green (130)
- yellow (97)

Stranded cotton (floss) colours
- dark purple (333)
- green (904)
- black (310)

Stitch guide (colours will vary)
- straight stitch
- ribbon stitch
- French knot (ribbon)
- lazy daisy (ribbon)
- spider web rose
- coral stitch
- bullion stitch
- French knot (stranded cotton – 6 strands)
- lazy daisy (stranded cotton – 3 strands)
- stem stitch (stranded cotton – 6 strands)

Corner motif

Posy

ring. Embroider the face using all six strands of the black embroidery thread in your embroidery needle.

{04} Complete the embroidery

Stitch all of the flower stems using six strands of green embroidery thread in your embroidery needle.

Working with the crewel needle, stitch the ribbon embroidered flowers surrounding the central flower and at the corners, using ribbon colours and widths as indicated. To get the most from your ribbon, stitch flowers of the same colour while you have the ribbon locked on to the needle. You may also find it easier to get into a rhythm of stitching all one type of flower before moving onto another. When working the spider web roses, work the base straight stitches with one strand of embroidery thread to match the ribbon colour.

Using three strands of purple embroidery thread, stitch the small lazy daisy flowers.

Stitch the posy border using the bright green 7mm ribbon in your chenille needle. Work two lazy daisy stitches for the top of the bow and two straight stitches for the tail ends.

{05} Make the table runner

Cut two pieces of yellow print fabric each measuring 15 x 45.5cm (6 x 18in). Pin and sew one piece to each end of the embroidered

linen, right sides facing. Cut the solid purple fabric to match the pieced top. With right sides facing, pin the purple backing fabric and runner top together. Sew around the runner, leaving a turning gap along one edge. Clip the corners, turn the runner right side out and sew the opening closed.

Using three strands of purple thread, sew a running stitch border around the edge of the runner and along the pieced seams of the top.

Embroidery Story

Ribbon embroidery isn't my typical stitching medium, but the fullness of the stitches is very appealing. However, it's so beautiful that I wasn't sure how to work that into my whimsical style! By using a few traditional embroidery stitches along with ribbon stitches, and taking a formal table runner and making it more casual, I was able to combine the styles into something that is both fun and fitting for ribbon embroidery.

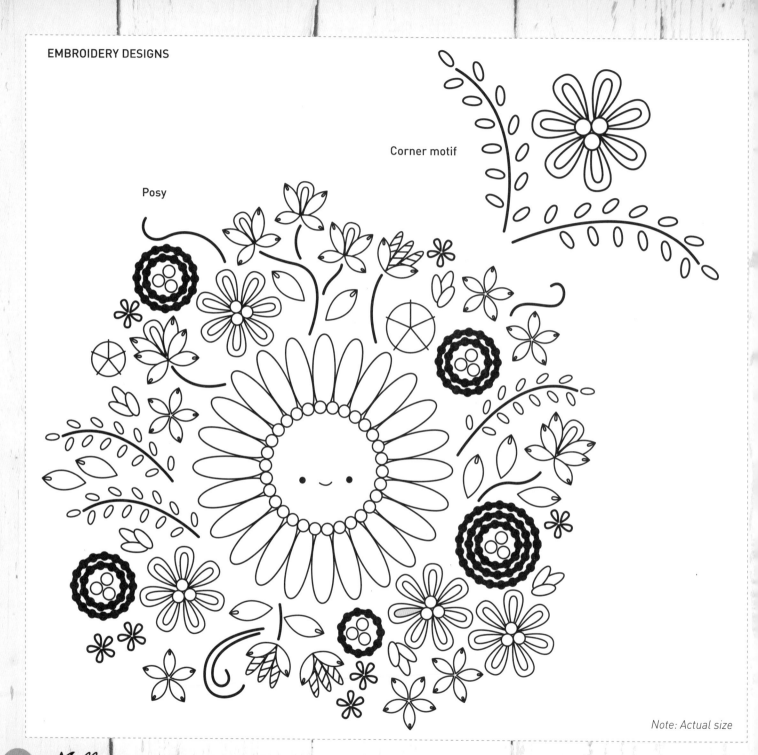

EMBROIDERY DESIGNS

Corner motif

Posy

Note: Actual size

Mama and baby owl ornaments

The mama and baby owl duo are perfect for decorating your desk or shelf. You'll learn lots of different ways to stitch feathers – from the minimalistic fern stitch to the fishbone stitch worked to look like a real feather! These owls are a great introduction to both basic and more advanced stitches.

MATERIALS

Two pieces of flax linen fabric, one piece 25 x 38cm (10 x 15in) and one piece 15 x 25cm (6 x 10in)

Stranded cotton (floss): black (DMC 310), copper orange (DMC 922), cream (DMC 945), dark brown (DMC 3031), light brown (DMC 3862), mid brown (DMC 975), white (DMC 3865)

Embroidery needles: size 9 and 10

Embroidery hoops: 18cm (7in) and 10cm (4in) diameter or larger

Polyester stuffing

Thin cardboard

SIZE

Finished owls: Mama 13cm (5¼in) tall; baby 7.5cm (3in) tall

STITCHES

Chain stitch (p. 97)
Buttonhole stitch (p. 98)
Satin stitch (p. 99)
Raised satin stitch (p. 99)
French knot (p. 100)
Straight stitch (p. 102)
Fern stitch (p. 105)
Fishbone stitch (p. 109)

FEATURED TECHNIQUES

- Using a hoop (p. 88)
- Transferring designs (p. 88)

MICHELLE GALLETTA

Michelle Galletta is a Toronto-based printmaker and embroidery enthusiast with a BFA from the Ontario College of Art and Design University. In 2012 she launched Kirikí Press, an indie design company that makes handcrafted embroidery kits, screen prints and other goods. Everything down to the packaging is printed and assembled by hand. Her line of products can be found at kirikipress.com.

METHOD

{01} Transfer the embroidery design

For the mama owl, cut a 25cm (10in) square from the larger piece of fabric and set aside the remainder to use for the backing later. For the baby owl cut a 15cm (6in) square from the smaller piece of fabric and again, set aside the remainder for the backing.

Using the light-box method and a fine-line pen in a shade slightly darker than the linen, transfer the mama and baby owl designs (p. 43) in the centre of the prepared linen fabric pieces, ensuring that the grain of the fabric is square to the pattern.

{02} Embroider the mama owl

Place the fabric in the large embroidery hoop, and stitch the embroidery using the thread colour and stitch diagram as your guide, working the design in the following order, using one strand of embroidery thread and size 10 needle unless specified otherwise.

Breast feathers: Work from bottom to top; work the buttonhole stitch as a scallop, keeping the stitches parallel to one another.

Wing feathers: Work from bottom to top. Note that the bottom-most feather at each side is worked in satin stitch, while all other feathers are worked in fishbone stitch. Slightly overlap the feathers as you embroider to avoid any fabric showing through.

Dots between breast feathers: Use two strands and size 9 needle.

Face outline: Use two strands and size 9 needle.

Facial features: Work the eyes, then the beak.

Decorative fill on head: Choose placement of the colours at random, but keep straight stitches consistent in length and space evenly.

Outline of owl: Use two strands and size 9 needle.

Once the embroidery is complete, leave the embroidered fabric in the hoop ready to make up the owl ornament as described in step 4.

{03} Embroider the baby owl

Place the fabric in the small embroidery hoop, and stitch the embroidery using the thread colour and stitch diagram (p. 42) as your guide, working the design in the following order, using the number of strands specified and a size 10 needle when working with one strand and size 9 for two strands.

Wing feathers: Work meandering lines using one strand.

Wing tips: Use two strands and work buttonhole stitches of increasing or decreasing length.

Wing outline: Use two strands.

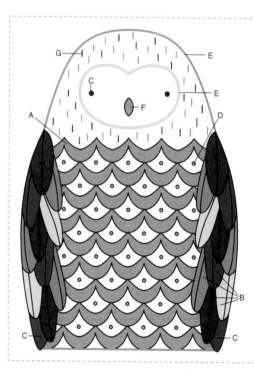

MAMA OWL THREAD COLOUR AND STITCH DIAGRAM

Note: 1 strand of DMC stranded cotton (floss) used unless specified otherwise

Stitches
A buttonhole stitch – 2 strands
B fishbone stitch
C satin stitch
D French knot – 2 strands
E chain stitch – 2 strands
F raised satin stitch
G straight stitch

Thread colours
◻ copper orange (922)
◼ black (310)
◻ cream (945)
◼ dark brown (3031)
◻ light brown (3862)
◼ mid brown (975)
◻ white (3865)

Embroidery Story

When I first learned to embroider, it was to make three soft toy owls for my niece. Owls have always been popular with embroiderers – the details on their feathers and adorable faces make them perfect for stitching. Bringing new life to a classic subject, I used a fresh illustrative style for my owls and designed the stitches to stylistically mimic feathers.

Breast feathers: Using two strands, work fern stitches of differing lengths, topping off each with a French knot.

Face outline: Use one strand.

Facial features: Work the eyes, then the beak, using one strand.

Decorative fill on body and head: Choose placement of the colours at random, but keep straight stitches consistent in length and space evenly; use one strand.

Outline of owl: Use two strands. Once the embroidery is complete, leave the embroidered fabric in the hoop ready to make up the owl ornament as described in step 4.

{04} Make the owl ornament

To make the backing, cut a rectangle of linen at least 1.3cm (½in) larger all around than the finished embroidered owl, taking care to make sure the grain of the fabric matches up.

Trace the mama or baby owl base template (see p. 157) onto a separate piece of linen and cut out along the dashed line. Trace the base (solid line only) onto a piece of thin cardboard, cut out and set aside.

Secure the relevant piece of the set-aside linen backing fabric evenly to the finished embroidery using pins or a tacking stitch. Turn the hoop over, so you can see the back of the embroidery. Use the reverse side of the owl outline chain stitch

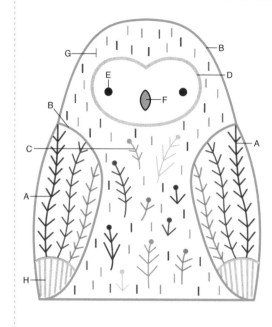

as your guide and sew as close to it as possible without sewing through any of the chain stitches, leaving the base unstitched and a gap for turning and stuffing as marked on the embroidery design. Remove the fabric from the hoop and cut around the owl shape allowing for a 6mm (¼in) seam allowance.

Sew the base in place so that the solid line marked on the template lines up to the chain stitched base of the owl. Turn the owl right side out. Insert the cardboard base through the turning/stuffing gap (you may have to bend it slightly to get it through), and position it so that it is completely flush along the base of

the owl. If it is too large, remove and trim as necessary. Stuff the owl until it is firm, then sew the gap closed using ladder stitch.

EMBROIDERY DESIGNS

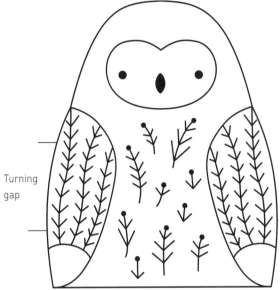

Turning
gap

Baby owl

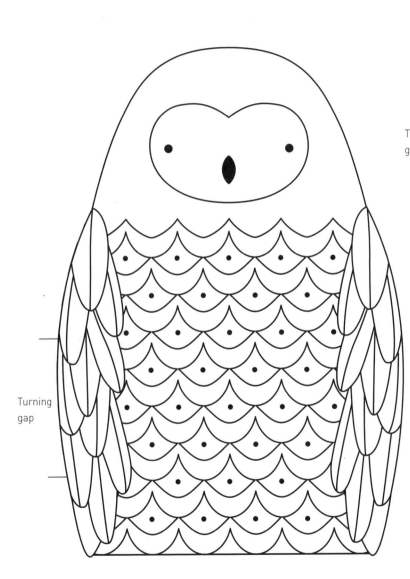

Turning
gap

Mama owl

Note: Actual size

Cross stitch iPhone covers

{ For a fast and functional no-sew project, use one of these bright and beautiful patterns to personalise a stitchable plastic phone case using the counted cross stitch technique. Choose between summery stripes and a perky little bird to make your mobile the best-dressed gadget in all the land.

MATERIALS

Stripe case

White stitchable plastic iPhone case (stitch size equivalent to 16-count Aida)

Stranded cotton (floss): aqua (DMC 959), olive (DMC 832), grey (DMC 645)

Bird case

Pink stitchable plastic iPhone case (stitch size equivalent to 16-count Aida)

Stranded cotton (floss): mid grey (DMC 645), dark grey (DMC 844), ecru (DMC ecru), black (DMC 310), mid olive (DMC 832), dark olive (DMC 831), light aqua (DMC 964), mid aqua (DMC 959)

Tapestry needle size 28

Small sharp scissors

Small pair of pliers (optional)

SIZE

Finished iPhone case: 6cm x 12.5cm (2⅜ x 5in)

STITCHES

Cross stitch (p. 94)

FEATURED TECHNIQUES

- Working from charted designs (p. 6)
- Counted cross stitch (p. 143)

Note

When stitching onto the plastic case you will need a smaller needle than you would usually use for stitching onto fabric of the same size because the holes in the plastic are quite small with very little give.

SOPHIE SIMPSON

Sophie is the designer, author and compulsive stitcher behind embroidery business, What Delilah Did. A perpetual dreamer and period drama-obsessive, she finds her happy place in rainy days, folk music and anything involving needles and yarn. When she's not making books you can find her tempting budding stitchers with imaginative patterns, exceptional embroidery kits and awesome workshops at whatdelilahdid.com.

Embroidery Story

The thing I love about this project is that there's nothing to do but to embroider it – the case is ready to use with no making up whatsoever! Working onto plastic takes a bit of getting used to, however, and if I did it all the time my fingers wouldn't thank me, but the result is really striking and super-practical to boot, so it was well worth the effort.

METHOD: STRIPE CASE

{01} Mark the centre point

To ensure the design is positioned in the middle of the case you need to begin by counting the size of the stitchable grid. Towards the middle of the case, count and note down the number of stitchable holes in one vertical line and one horizontal line (if you count lines near the edge, the number will not be accurate as the corners of the grid are rounded). The number of stitches you can fit onto your grid in each direction equals the number of holes minus one: the cases we have used have 37 stitchable holes in one direction and 80 stitchable holes in the other, which means that the stitchable grid measures 36 x 79 stitches. The size of your grid may differ slightly depending on your case.

Divide the number of stitches (not the number of holes) in each direction by two, and note down these numbers. To find the vertical centre line, take the halved number of stitches in a horizontal line and count that many holes from the left-hand edge, ignoring the first hole. So for our case:

36 horizontal stitches ÷ 2 = 18 sts

The hole you land on is where you put the vertical centre line. Using any thread, quickly sew a running stitch along this vertical line (there is no need to secure the ends), keeping the stitches quite long so that they are easy to unpick later.

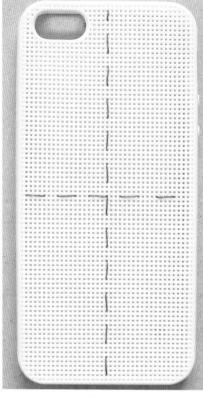

Marking the centre point.

Repeat the process in the opposite direction to find the horizontal centre line. If your line should fall between two holes (as our horizontal line does), pick either one making a note of the side you chose so that you remember where the exact centre point is when you come to start stitching (for example, we picked the hole/line below). The two lines you have stitched correspond to the two centre lines on the chart (see Working from Charted Designs, p. 6).

Note

If you have a smaller phone case, by working from the centre of the design you can be sure that the pattern will still look well placed even if some of the edges are cut short.

{02} Begin with a knotless loop start

It is important to keep the reverse of the stitching as flat as possible so that the phone sits snugly in the case, so use a knotless loop start. Cut a length of embroidery thread about 60cm (23¾in) long, separate a single strand, fold the strand in half and thread the two loose ends through the eye of the needle. Count from the centre point to the start of the section where you want to begin stitching and begin the stitch at its bottom left-hand corner. When making your first half stitch, leave some thread (the end with the loop) at the back of the case, then pass the needle and thread through this loop (see below) and pull closed to secure the thread without a knot.

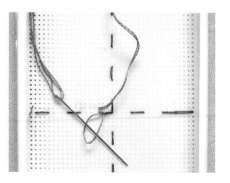

{03} Embroider the design

Using the stripe chart for reference (p. 49), count the stitches (and gaps) in the colour you are using from your starting point to the right-hand side, completing half stitches all along the row and then going back to 'cross' all the stitches from right to left. Once you have the first few stitches in place you can unpick the centre lines.

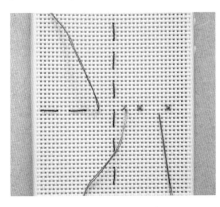

Continue working downwards in rows, completing all of the nearby stitches in the colour you are using. When you come to the end of a thread, secure it without a knot by running the needle underneath a few stitches on the reverse and snip off the loose end.

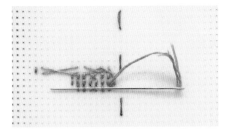

When you reach the bottom of a section, turn the case and chart upside down and stitch the rest of the section downwards in rows as before. Move around each section to complete all the stitches in the colour you are using, counting the placement of stitches and spaces in relation to those already completed.

Once all of one colour has been completed in a section, move on to the next colour. Move around the pattern, working each section from the centre outwards and turning the case upside down when necessary to complete different sections.

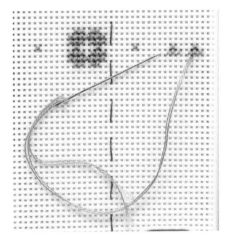

Note

Always turn the case 180 degrees in either direction to ensure all of the top legs of your cross stitches face in the same direction – if you turn the case to the side the stitches will end up facing the other way and this can look messy.

Finishing at the corners: The case is a little flexible, so generally you can bend back the edges to get the needle out when finishing off threads. However, as this is not possible at the corners, you should carry the thread to fasten it behind stitches on a couple of different rows for extra security. (In particularly awkward sections, use a small pair of pliers to help you pull out the needle.)

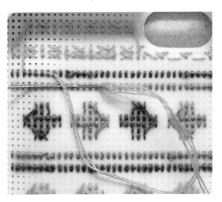

Accommodating the camera hole: A full chart has been provided to accommodate different-sized phone cases, and you will need to miss out the relevant sections when you get to the camera hole, stitching around it as closely as you can to continue the pattern.

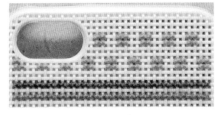

METHOD: BIRD CASE

{01} Mark the centre point
As stripe case, step 1 (p. 46).

{02} Begin with a knotless loop start
As stripe case, step 2 (p. 46).

{03} Embroider the design
Follow the bird chart opposite: start near the centre point to complete half stitches for the mid grey in the first row, then go back along the row crossing the stitches. Once you have the first few stitches in place, unpick the centre lines (photo, below).

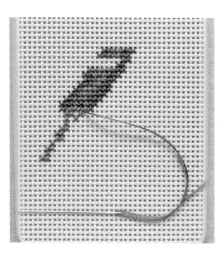

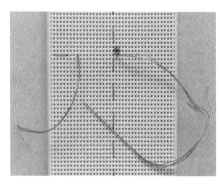

Continue working downwards in rows, completing all of that section's stitches in the colour you are using. When you come to the end of a thread, remember to secure it without a knot by running the needle underneath a few stitches on the reverse of the case and snipping off the loose end. Next stitch the dark grey area around the stitches you have just completed, starting at the top of the section and working down in rows (photo, top left).

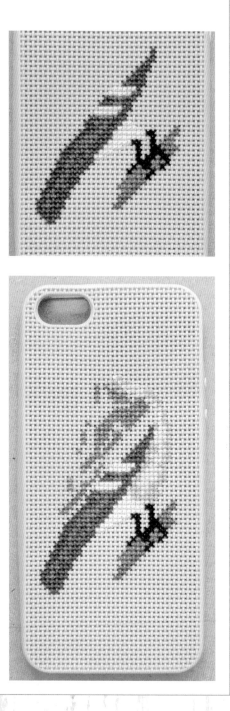

When you reach the bottom of a section, turn the case and chart upside down and stitch the rest of the section downwards in rows as before. Move around the pattern, completing all of the same colour stitches in a section before moving on to the next. Flip the case and pattern 180 degrees where necessary, working downwards in rows throughout. We stitched the subsequent sections in the following order:
Ecru.
Black feet.
Mid olive and dark olive branch (photo, top right).
Light aqua inner belly.
Mid aqua outer belly.
Mid olive inner wing (photo, right).
Dark olive outer wing.
Mid grey head.
Black beak and eye.
Dark grey head.

CHARTED DESIGNS

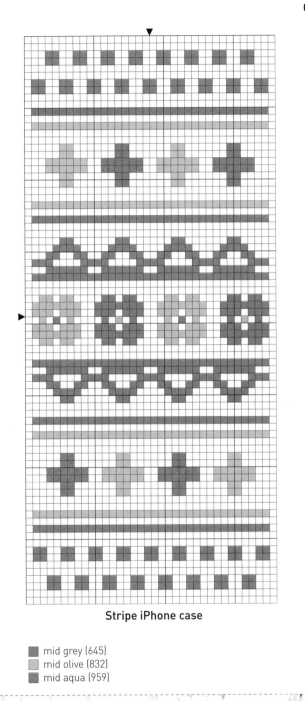

Stripe iPhone case

- ■ mid grey (645)
- ■ mid olive (832)
- ■ mid aqua (959)

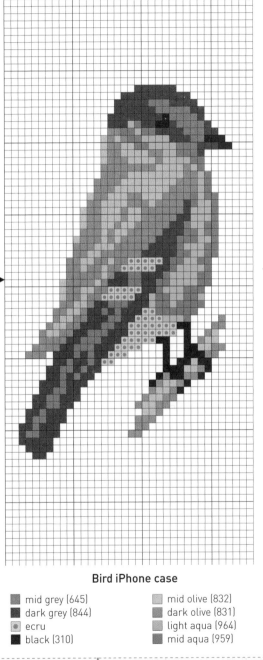

Bird iPhone case

- ■ mid grey (645)
- ■ dark grey (844)
- ● ecru
- ■ black (310)
- ■ mid olive (832)
- ■ dark olive (831)
- ■ light aqua (964)
- ■ mid aqua (959)

Busy bee Kindle case

Decorated with colourful crewel embroidered flowers and a bumblebee in flight, this felt cover will protect your e-reader in style! The wool felt fabric is so easy to embroider that there is no need to use a hoop, and it will cushion your Kindle when you toss it in your bag.

MATERIALS

Two pieces of olive green craft-weight wool felt each 16.5 x 23cm (6½ x 9in)

Appletons 2-ply crewel wool: yellow (844), black (993), creamy white (873), hot pink (945), light pink (754), green (426)

Metallic stranded cotton (floss): iridescent white (DMC E200)

Crewel needle size 5–10

Sewing thread to match felt

Pinking shears

SIZE

Finished cover: 15 x 21.5cm (6 x 8½in)

STITCHES

Chain stitch (p. 97)
Raised satin stitch (p. 99)
French knot (p. 100)
Split stitch (p. 103)
Cloud filling stitch (p. 137)

FEATURED TECHNIQUES

- Transferring designs (p. 88)
- Crewelwork embroidery (p. 136)

Note

This project is sized for a Kindle Fire, which measures 19 x 12cm (7½ x 4¾in) with a depth of 1.2cm (approx ½in). To make a pattern to fit your e-reader, trace around it onto a piece of paper and add the depth measurement plus a seam allowance of 1.5cm (⅝in) to each side; use the pattern to cut two pieces from your wool felt.

EMILY BAIER

Emily has been playing with fibre and getting messy with paint her entire life. Having gained a BFA in photography and printmaking from Savannah College of Art and Design, she started her business, Tako Fibers, designing and producing crewel embroidery kits for all skill levels. She lives in Portland, Oregon with her family and excessive collection of crafting supplies. To find out more, visit takofibers.com.

METHOD

{01} Transfer the embroidery design

Transfer the embroidery design onto one piece of the wool felt – if working with a dark coloured felt, the best method to use is the tearaway stabiliser method (see p. 88). (For light coloured felt, trace the design directly onto the wool felt using the carbon paper transfer method.) Pin the stabiliser transfer to one piece of the felt, making sure that the bee is centred.

{02} Embroider the bee

Referring to the detail photograph of the bee, begin to embroider the design. Using one strand of black yarn, work the outline of the bee's head and the outline of the second and the fourth stripes with split stitch, then fill in with raised satin stitch, taking care to stitch over the edge of the split stitch outlines. Use split stitch to make the legs and the antennae. At the end of each antenna, make a small French knot.

Working with one strand of yellow yarn, outline the first and third stripes of the bee with split stitch, then fill in with raised satin stitch, taking care to end your stitches where the black stripes begin. After the bee is filled in, make lines of split stitch between each stripe with the yellow yarn.

Using one strand of creamy white yarn, outline the wings of the bee with split stitch, and complete

stage one of the cloud filling infill by working very small straight stitches diagonally across the wings as indicated by the dots marked on the embroidery design.

Changing to two strands of metallic thread in your needle, complete stage two of the cloud filling infill (see step 1, p. 137), weaving the metallic threads between the straight stitches. Work each row individually, working from one side of the inner edge of the split stitch outline to the other. Secure the metallic thread at the beginning and end of each row by tucking the thread under the straight stitches on the reverse of the work.

{03} Embroider the flowers

With one strand of green yarn, stitch each flower stem using chain stitch. Continuing with the green yarn, outline each leaf with split stitch, then make several small lines of split stitch to fill in the leaves.

Beginning with the hot pink flowers and referring to the photograph of the finished embroidery on p. 51 for their placement, use one strand of hot pink to outline the flowers with split stitch then carefully fill in each flower with satin stitch, stitching over the outline, taking particular care at the points of each flower. Repeat for the light pink flowers.

 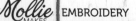

{04} Finish the embroidery

Secure and trim any long threads on the back of your piece. Gently tear away the excess stabiliser, using a pair of tweezers to gently pull the stabiliser from the more delicate parts of the stitching if necessary.

{05} Make the Kindle case

Place the embroidered felt right side up on top of the second piece of felt, aligning the edges. Machine stitch a 1.5cm (⅝in) seam around the edges, pivoting at the corners and leaving the top edge open. Trim the fabric to 6mm (¼in) from the stitching line using pinking shears. Slip the Kindle inside the cover. It will fit very snugly at first, but it will stretch to fit your device perfectly.

Embroidery Story

After collecting and admiring vintage crewel embroidery pieces for years, I decided to try to convert some of my own illustrations using this technique. I taught myself the basics from books, and now share what I have learnt by making my own crewel embroidery kits for beginners and advanced stitchers. I especially love crewel embroidery for the incredibly textured and colourful surfaces – it looks like a painting made with yarn.

EMBROIDERY DESIGN

Note: Actual size

Kitty cats tea cosy

This double-sided tea cosy is a fun way to keep your teapot warm. One side is decorated with a pretty kitty (see p. 57) and the other with a very suave tom cat. The designs are built up by appliquéing fabrics, which are then embroidered with a wonderful mix of hand and free-motion machine embroidery.

MATERIALS

One piece of floral print cotton and one piece of royal blue wool felt each 35 x 30cm (13¾ x 11¾in) for the tea cosy backgrounds

One piece of cotton approx 60 x 60cm (23¾ x 23¾in) for the lining

One piece of grey felt approx 22 x 10cm (8¾ x 4in) for boy cat appliqué

One piece of apricot felt approx 15 x 10cm (6 x 4in) for girl cat appliqué

Fabric scraps for appliqué decoration: red felt, peach felt, green printed fabric, pink polka dot fabric, striped fabric, white cotton

Sewing threads: black, red, white, dark grey, pale pink

Stranded cotton (floss): white (DMC blanc), black (DMC 310), grey (DMC 3799), pale pink (DMC 3326), dark pink (DMC 601), dark apricot (DMC 3856)

Darner needle size 1–5

Embroidery hoop 13cm (5in) diameter

Piece of trim for tab approx 10cm (4in) long

Lightweight wadding approx 60cm (23¾in) square

A4 sheet of double-sided fusible webbing

Small button

SIZE

Finished cosy: approx 28 x 25cm (11 x 10in)

STITCHES

Chain stitch (p. 97)
Lazy daisy (see detached chain stitch, p. 97)
Satin stitch (p. 99)
Straight stitch (p. 102)

FEATURED TECHNIQUES

- Transferring designs (p. 88)
- Free-motion machine embroidery (p. 150)

METHOD

{01} Cut the fabrics for the tea cosy

Transfer the tea cosy template on p. 158 onto a folded sheet of A3 paper and cut out to make a tea cosy pattern. Use the pattern to cut two tea cosy shapes from the lining fabric, two from the wadding and one from each of the two tea cosy background fabrics.

{02} Cut the appliqué pieces

Use the appliqué templates on p. 158 to draw two pairs of cat's eyes, two cat bodies, one dress, hair bow, neck tie and beret onto the paper side of the fusible webbing, paper side up and roughly cut out the shapes. Place the cut out shapes on the wrong side of the relevant fabric and heat-fix with an iron using a pressing cloth to get a really good bond. Once the fabric has cooled, cut around the drawn outlines using sharp embroidery scissors. Remove the paper backing.

EMBROIDERY DESIGN

Note: Actual size

{03} Attach the main appliqué pieces onto the background fabrics

Arrange the grey cat's body centrally onto the royal blue felt tea cosy shape, fusible webbing side down; when you are happy with the position, lay the pressing cloth over the top and press with a hot iron to bond. Attach the neck tie in the same way. Repeat to fix the apricot cat's body onto the floral print tea cosy shape, and the dress on top of that. Fix one pair of eyes to each cat's face in the same way. To secure the appliqué pieces in place, machine stitch around the outline of the cats, their clothes and their eyes, taking your time and using your fingers to gently manoeuvre around the pieces.

{04} Transfer and embroider the pattern for the girl's face

Using the cat's face embroidery design opposite as your guide, mark out the facial details onto the girl cat's face using a water-soluble pen. Use three strands of black embroidery thread to work the pupils in satin stitch. Work a few straight stitches at the top edge of the eye for the eyelashes. Using three strands of dark apricot embroidery thread, work chain stitch for the eyebrow/nose line. Use three strands of pale pink embroidery thread to work the satin stitch triangle for the nose tip. Work three lazy daisy stitch flowers with all six strands of white embroidery thread to create the collar at the top edge of the striped fabric dress.

Machine stitch the marked guidelines for the mouth using black sewing thread, making a little backwards and forwards stitch at the mouth edges to create a little detail.

For the cheek detailing, work straight stitches using dark pink embroidery thread to produce a star pattern over small dark pink felt circles. Sew the small button 'brooch' onto the top right of the dress.

{05} Transfer and embroider the design for the boy's face and body

Follow the instructions in step 4 to embroider the boy's face with the following amendments:

omit the eyelashes and work the pupils looking to the left; use grey embroidery thread for the eyebrow/nose line and black embroidery thread for the nose tip. When machine stitching the mouth, make the shape a little less curvy. For the cheek detailing, work straight stitches using white cotton thread to produce a star pattern over small pink felt circles.

To create 'fur' detail, work small straight stitches beneath the neck tie using dark grey embroidery thread.

{06} Add detailing with free-motion embroidery

Place your embroidery in the hoop and set your machine for free-motion embroidery (see p. 150). 'Draw' some texture lines onto the cats' faces, along the brow and at the base of each ear, using pink sewing thread for the girl and grey for the boy. Once the free-motion embroidery is complete, the final appliqué pieces – kitty's hair bow and tom cat's beret – can be bonded and machine stitched in place.

{07} Make a tea cosy sandwich

Fold the small piece of trim in half and pin centrally at the top of one of the cosy fronts, right side facing up. Place the cosy fronts together, right sides facing. Sandwich the fronts between the two pieces of wadding and pin. Machine stitch around the outer edge of the layered fabrics, flattening the wadding as you go to ensure it does not get caught in the feed dogs or needle, and taking care to keep your fingers clear of the needle. Set aside.

SAMANTHA STAS

Two morning lattes, *Women's Hour* and full make-up – that's how Samantha makes working from home work for her. With two small children, she is the first to admit that it can be hard to juggle everything, but she wouldn't change what she does for the world. She finds inspiration from vintage children's books, retro fabrics and all things nostalgic. To see what she is doing and say hello pop over to etsy.com/shop/samanthastas.

{08} Make the lining

Take the two lining pieces and place together with right sides facing, and machine stitch around the curved edge approx 6mm (¼in) in from the edge, leaving a gap at the top just large enough for your hand to fit through – approx 8cm (3⅛in) for turning the cosy out later. Turn the sewn lining so that the right sides are on the outside, and place this inside your set-aside tea cosy sandwich, taking care to line up the lining seams with the cosy seams (if necessary, make any adjustments by trimming to fit before stitching). Keeping the pieces together, machine stitch around the bottom raw edges 6mm (¼in) in, watching out for your needle going over any 'lumpy' seams and using your fingers to help flatten as you sew.

{09} Turn through and finish

Find the opening in the lining and pull your tea cosy through, using your fingers to help create a nice curve. When you are happy with the shape, sew the lining opening closed before pushing the lining back up into the tea cosy, using your fingers to 'roll' the bottom of the cosy so that the joined fabrics sit well. Machine stitch along the bottom edge, approx 6mm (¼in) in, keeping an eye out for the bulky seams. Now all you need to do is to give your tea cosy a final press and put the kettle on.

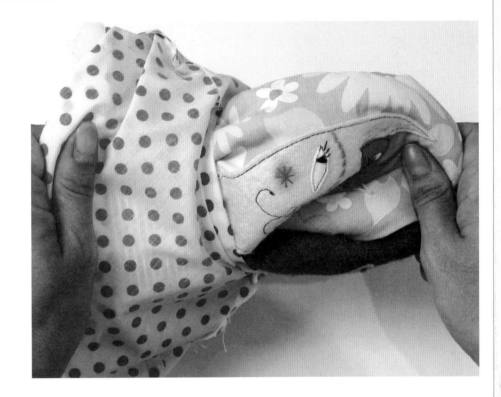

Embroidery Story

Machine embroidery gives me instant satisfaction. It's lovely to sit and tinker with some hand embroidery, but I find nothing beats the quick effects that can be achieved with the machine. I used to draw a lot as a child, and it is that same sense of mark-making onto fabric that I love about free-motion machine embroidery. You can literally scribble a design on paper, make up some templates and off you go. Don't get disheartened if your first attempts aren't what you wanted – in my experience, those little imperfections just add to the overall effect. The beauty is, there are no rules!

Ladybird needlework set

There are many ways to make your embroidery stand out. Ribbon embroidery and beads can add texture, but for truly eye-popping dimensions, try a little raised work. Simple stumpwork techniques are used for the flowers and larger-than-life ladybird on this little needlework set.

MATERIALS

Linen: two pieces 30.5cm (12in) square for the needle book; one piece 38cm (15in) square for the pincushion

Stranded cotton (floss): black (DMC 310), light green (DMC 469), mid green (DMC 470), dark green (DMC 471), brown (DMC 611), red (DMC 3831), white (DMC blanc), gold metallic (DMC E3852), variegated purple (DMC 4220)

Embroidery needle size 10

Embroidery hoop 25cm (10in) diameter

One piece of printed cotton fabric 25 x 20.5cm x (10 x 8in)

One piece of white felt 15 x 7.5cm (6 x 3in)

Small pieces of light blue and pink felt and green fabric

Two small buttons

Strong thread

Pipe cleaner

Polyester filling

STITCHES

Stem stitch (p. 96)
Detached chain stitch (p. 97)
Buttonhole stitch (p. 98)
Raised satin stitch (p. 99)
French knot (p. 100)
Whipped chain stitch (p. 133)

SIZE

Finished needle book: 9 x 9cm (3½ x 3½in)
Finished pincushion: 7.5cm (3in) diameter

FEATURED TECHNIQUES

- Using a hoop (p. 88)
- Transferring designs (p. 88)

EMILY WILMARTH

Emily was introduced to fibre crafts early by her mother, leading to a lifelong interest in needlework, but she only started embroidery just a few years ago, having been inspired by a book featuring stumpwork projects. Living in Sweden's countryside provides Emily with constant inspiration for natural themes, which often find their way into her work. You can find out more at The Floss Box, theflossbox.com.

METHOD

{01} Prepare and start to embroider the needle book design

Transfer the needle book embroidery design (including the outline shape of the needle book) to one of the 30.5cm (12in) linen squares. Lay the linen over the second 30.5cm (12in) linen square and place it in the hoop – the second piece of linen acts as a backing fabric to give the needle book more firmness and the two fabrics become sewn together as you embroider. *(Note: The needle book shape is not cut out until the design is embroidered.)*

Referring to the photo of the needle book embroidery design opposite, start the embroidery. Using three strands of mid green thread (DMC 470), chain stitch the main vine. Whip the chain stitch with two strands of light green thread (DMC 469). Embroider the remaining stems with stem stitch and two strands of light green thread.

The three small leaves are stitched with raised satin stitch using one strand of dark green thread (DMC 471). Make several long straight stitches along the length of the leaf either side of the centre line,

then stitch angled satin stitches to each side. Stitch the centre line with small backstitches using one strand of light green thread (DMC 469).

Stitch the tendrils with stem stitch using one strand of dark green thread (DMC 471).

Note

Stumpwork, popular in 17th century England, uses several techniques to create raised surfaces and free-standing elements. Paddings, slips (pieces of embroidered fabric sewn onto main fabric) and wires raise and shape to add dimension.

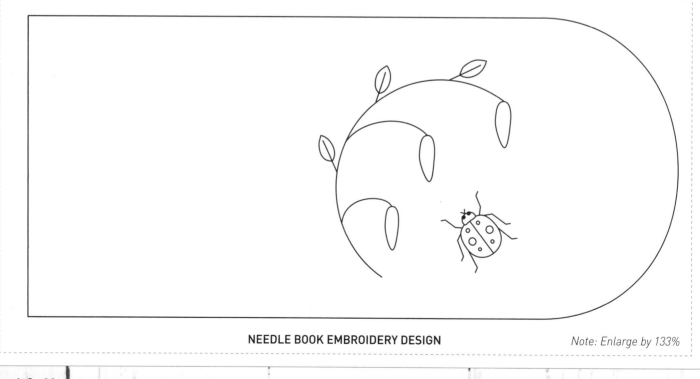

NEEDLE BOOK EMBROIDERY DESIGN

Note: Enlarge by 133%

{02} Embroider the wisteria flower clusters

These are worked at the end of each of the stems. Use the wisteria padding template on p. 156 to cut out three shapes from the light blue felt. Positioning one at the end of each stem, stab stitch all around the edge of the felt shape to secure it in place. Cover the felt shape with French knots using three strands of variegated purple thread (DMC 4220). To make sure there is good colour variation over the flower, cut three lengths of thread for each flower, and take one strand from each into your needle. To create a nice shape to the cluster, make the French knots around the edge of the felt first, then fill in.

At the top of each flower cluster work a detached chain stitch leaf at either side using one strand of dark green thread (DMC 471) and one strand of mid green thread (DMC 470) in the needle.

{03} Embroider the ladybird

Cut out the three ladybird padding templates on p. 156 from pink felt. Starting with the smallest piece and ending with the largest, stab stitch down the three layers of felt, working around the edge of each to secure in place. Using one strand of red thread (DMC 3831), work satin stitch along the length of the ladybird's body over the felt layers.

Make the centre line of the body with one straight stitch using one strand of black thread (DMC 310). The ladybird's head is worked with raised satin stitch: make horizontal stitches for the first layer, then vertical stitches for the top layer. Work straight stitches for the antennae. Work French knots for the eyes using one strand of white (DMC blanc) thread. Work French knots for the ladybird's spots using two strands of black thread, but be sure not to pull too hard on the thread as you do not want the knots to sink into the body. Fill any gaps in the satin stitch on the ladybird's body with straight stitches using one strand of red thread. Work the legs with straight stitch using one strand of the gold metallic thread (DMC E3852).

Stitches that add texture and relief are featured in stumpwork, and can include bullion stitch, French knots, raised satin stitch and other types of raised stitches. Stitches are often worked over padding, as in the wisteria and ladybird body.

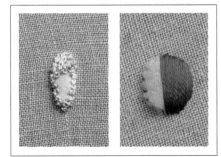

{04} Make the needle book

Use the templates on p. 156 to cut one of each of the needle book lining patterns from your printed cotton fabric. Place together with right sides facing, aligning the straight edges, and stitch with a 6mm (¼in) seam allowance, sewing from each edge towards the centre, but leaving an opening (a turning gap) in the middle as marked.

Make the button loop. Cut a strip of lining fabric measuring 2.5 x 10cm (1 x 4in). Fold in half with wrong sides facing so that the long edges align, and press. Fold the raw edges back to the centre fold line, then fold the fabric strip along the original fold so that right sides are facing and the raw edges are encased within. Sew the strip together along the edge. At the centre point of the folded

fabric strip, fold back each end at a 45-degree angle to create the end of the loop, making sure the loop is big enough to pass your button through. Attach the folded strip to the right side of the lining fabric in the centre of the rounded flap, with the folded tip facing inwards.

Remove the embroidered fabric from the hoop and cut out on the marked line for the shape of the needle book cover. Place the lining fabric and the embroidered fabric together with right sides facing and sew all the way around the edge with a 6mm (¼in) seam allowance. Trim the corners and cut notches in the rounded area, then turn right side out through the gap in the lining. Carefully press the needle book avoiding the embroidered area, and sew the opening closed. Fold the white felt in half and sew it along the lining seam.

Fold up the needle book and mark the placement for the button. Sew the button to the front of the flap, catching a tiny bit of the lining fabric in the needle as you go. Work the buttonhole stitch edging all around the outside of the needle book using one strand of the metallic gold thread.

{05} Prepare and embroider the pincushion design

Mark the pincushion embroidery design (including the outline shape of the panel) five times onto the remaining piece of linen, laying them out with a row of three, then two below, so that the two rows overlap to make the most economic use of the fabric. Place the fabric in a hoop and begin the embroidery. First work the central stems with stem stitch using two strands of light green thread (DMC 469), then the tendrils again with stem stitch using one strand of dark green thread (DMC 471). Embroider the wisteria flower clusters at the end of each

of the central stems as described in step 2, but use one strand of light green thread (DMC 469) and one strand of mid green thread (DMC 470) when stitching the two detached chain stitch leaves.

{06} Make the pincushion

Use the pincushion leaf template on p. 156 to cut out two leaves from the green fabric. Place together with wrong sides facing and sew around the edge with a 6mm (¼in) seam leaving the base open; turn the leaf right side out through the opening. Press, then fold the leaf in half lengthways from the bottom through the narrow part of the leaf only.

Remove the embroidered fabric from the hoop and cut out the five embroidered sections. Stitch the sections together using a 6mm (¼in) seam allowance, beginning and ending your stitching at the marked dots. When sewing in the final section, line the base of the leaf

Embroidery Story

I find that stumpwork is well-suited to capturing the beauty of the natural world. Flowers, insects and small animals are traditional subjects. The wisteria's beautiful colours and hanging flowers and vines inspired this needlework. Ladybirds have a delightful round form that is created with the help of stumpwork techniques. The needle book design can also be framed or finished in many other ways.

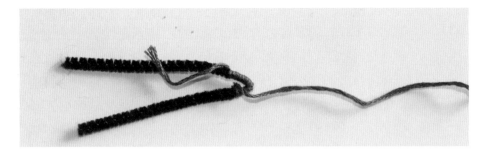

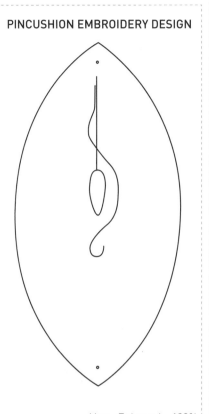

Note: Enlarge by 133%

up at the top of the apple with the leaf pointing downwards. Sew the final seam, leaving a small opening at the bottom, and turn the apple right side out.

To make the stem, cut a 10cm (4in) piece of pipe cleaner. Fold it in half, then unfold. Begin wrapping the pipe cleaner with brown thread (DMC 611) using all six strands, starting just before the middle, then working your way over to the other side of the centre point.

Fold the pipe cleaner in half again and, holding it together tightly, continue to wrap the thread over the doubled up pipe cleaner until the wrapped section measures about 3.2cm (1¼in). Tie a knot, then cut the thread leaving a tail of at least 15cm (6in). Push the stem into the top of the pincushion so only the wrapped section can be seen, and bring the thread tail to the inside and secure. Sew closed any gaps in the seams around the stem using small stitches. Stuff the apple with the polyester filling until it is nice and firm, then sew the turning gap closed.

Thread a long needle with the strong doubled over thread. Pull the needle through one of the seams bringing it out at the base of the apple, so that the knot fastens inside the apple. Sew on the button, bringing the needle through the apple and up at the top. Stitch back and forth through the apple a few times, pulling on the thread as you do so to make a good apple shape. Take a couple of tiny stitches under the button to anchor the thread and bring the needle out through one of the apple seams so that when you cut the thread the ends will disappear into the body of the apple.

Alphabet sampler picture

This A to Z is stitched in a rainbow of colours and it is the perfect project for you to sample many stitches from across all seven of the stitch families featured in the Techniques section. Stitch all 26 letters to make a picture, or use individual letters to make your mark.

MATERIALS

One piece of white cotton fabric 38 x 45.5cm (15 x 18in)

Stranded cotton (floss): light pink (DMC 151), dark pink (DMC 601), dark orange (DMC 720), mid orange (DMC 721), light orange (DMC 722), light yellow (DMC 745), mid yellow (DMC 726), dark yellow (DMC 725), dark green (DMC 699), mid green (DMC 703), light green (DMC 704), dark blue (DMC 336), mid blue (DMC 826), light blue (DMC 827), dark purple (DMC 333), mid purple (DMC 340), light purple (DMC 210)

Embroidery needle size 5

Two sheets of Sulky Sticky Fabri-Solvy

Large Q-Snap embroidery frame

Framing materials: foam-core board 28 x 35.5cm (11 x 14in), straight pins, strong thread, frame to fit (optional)

SIZE

Finished picture: 28 x 35.5cm (11 x 14in)

STITCHES

Backstitch (p. 92)
Stem stitch (p. 96)
Chain stitch (p. 97)
Detached chain stitch (p. 97)
Satin stitch (p. 99)
Raised satin stitch (p. 99)
French knot (p. 100)
Split stitch (p. 103)
Double running stitch (p. 104)
Fern stitch (p. 105)
Seed stitch (p. 105)
Fishbone stitch (p. 109)
Encroaching satin stitch (p. 110)
St George's cross stitch (p. 111)
Star filling stitch (p. 112)
Zigzag stitch (p. 113)
Chinese knot (p. 115)

FEATURED TECHNIQUES

- Using a hoop (p. 88)
- Transferring designs (p. 88)

Scroll stitch (p. 119)
Knotted buttonhole stitch (p. 120)
Loop stitch (p. 122)
Open chain stitch (p. 126)
Whipped running stitch (p. 132)
Whipped satin stitch (p. 132)
Whipped chain stitch (p. 133)
Threaded backstitch (p. 134)
Double threaded backstitch (p. 134)
Threaded detached chain stitch (p. 135)
Threaded herringbone stitch (p. 135)

METHOD

{01} Prepare your fabric and threads

Prewash your fabric to remove any sizing. Don't use fabric softener in the rinse – it can keep your stabiliser from sticking properly. Press the fabric once it is dry.

{02} Transfer the embroidery design

To make the picture as shown, the embroidery design needs to be enlarged (see p. 70). Print or copy the embroidery design onto the Sulky Sticky Fabri-Solvy (a pattern transfer and stabiliser in one), printing the top on one sheet and the bottom on the second sheet. Peel off the backing and stick the pattern transfer/stabiliser to the fabric, overlapping as necessary (see photo below).

{03} Embroider the design

Place your fabric in the frame, and embroider the design as follows.

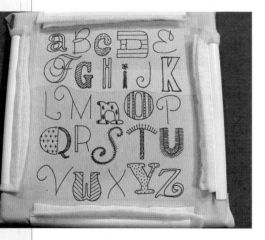

Note: All stitches are worked in 4 strands of thread unless otherwise specified. For each letter, stitches are listed in the order worked.

Letter A: Outline – backstitch in dark pink (601), centre line – backstitch in light purple (210) working French knots in dark purple (333) between backstitches.

Letter B: Whipped running stitch – work running stitch in mid blue (826) with whipping in light orange (722).

Letter C: Outline – backstitch in mid yellow (726), infill – seed stitch in dark yellow (725), light yellow (745) and light green (704).

Letter D: Encroaching satin stitch worked in alternating stripes of dark purple (333) and mid purple (340).

Letter E: Double running stitch worked in dark blue (336) and mid orange (721).

Letter F: Satin stitch the wide bits, stem stitch the skinny bits, all in mid green (703).

Letter G: Outline – backstitch in mid orange (721), stripes – threaded backstitch with backstitch worked in mid orange (721) and whipped in mid yellow (726).

Letter H: Open chain stitch in dark purple (333).

Letter I: Flower – detached chain stitch in 2 strands of dark orange (720) with French knot centre in 2 strands of dark yellow (725), stalk –

fishbone stitch in 2 strands of dark green (699).

Letter J: Threaded detached chain stitch with chains worked in 2 strands of dark pink (601) and threading loops worked in 4 strands of dark yellow (725).

Letter K: Raised satin stitch in mid blue (826), outlined with backstitch in mid green (703) with French knots between each backstitch.

Letter L: Double threaded backstitch – work backstitch in dark yellow (725) and thread with mid orange (721) and dark pink (601).

Letter M: Whipped running stitch – work running stitch in mid purple (340) with whipping in dark blue (336).

Letter N: Outline – backstitch in dark pink (601), infill – star stitch in 2 strands of dark yellow (725).

Letter O: Outline – backstitch in dark blue (336), stripes – backstitch in 2 strands of light green (704), dots – Chinese knots in 2 strands of light green (704).

Letter P: Backstitched chain stitch with chain stitch in mid orange (721) and backstitch in dark purple (333).

Letter Q: Outline – backstitch, infill left (fat) side – St George's cross stitch, infill right (skinny) side – satin stitch. All worked in mid blue (826).

Letter R: Wide stem – threaded herringbone stitch with herringbone worked in 2 strands of mid orange

(721), threading in 2 strands of light pink (151), rest of letter – split stitch with 4 strands of mid orange (721).

Letter S: Fern stitch in 2 strands of mid green (703).

Letter T: Top arc – knotted buttonhole in light orange (722), stem of letter – zigzag stitch also light orange (722).

WENDI GRATZ

Wendi Gratz is incapable of watching television without an embroidery hoop, needle and thread in her hands, and will happily stitch for hours on end while watching marathons of her favourite shows. She loves colour, pattern, fake fur and monsters. She designs embroidery, sewing and quilting patterns especially for beginners and has a website loaded with video tutorials at ShinyHappyWorld.com.

Embroidery Story

Designing an alphabet sampler made up of beautiful letters filled with lots of different patterns was my dream project as it gave me a chance to explore my love of pattern – stripes and plaids and dots and zigzags! One of the most satisfying parts of any embroidery project is finishing it, and in a project like this you get the satisfaction of finishing 26 different times.

Letter U: Loop stitch in 2 strands of mid purple (340).

Letter V: Centre line – split stitch in light orange (722), row either side of centre line – split stitch in dark orange (720).

Letter W: Whipped satin stitch – work raised satin stitch in dark purple (333) with whipping in 2 strands of mid green (703).

Letter X: Whipped chain stitch with chain stitch in 3 strands of dark yellow (725) and whipping in mid blue (826).

Letter Y: Outline – scroll stitch in dark blue (336), infill – French knots in mid blue (826).

Letter Z: Raised satin stitch in dark pink (601), outlined with chain stitch in mid green (703).

{04} Prepare for framing

Rinse away the stabiliser in cool water – change your water frequently and rinse the fabric really well from both sides to be sure you get it all out especially around the very dense stitching. Lay your embroidery face down on a thick, colourfast towel. Smooth it out and carefully press it dry, working from the centre to the edges and on the back only.

Centre your embroidery over the foam-core board. Insert flat-headed straight pins into the sides of the board at the mid-point of each side, making sure that everything is straight and centred. Stand the board on its edge, pull the fabric taut, smoothing without stretching, and pin in place every couple of centimetres or so into the edge of the board. Check again that everything is straight and centred before framing, if you choose to. Alternatively, use a bulldog clip to hang the finished sampler.

EMBROIDERY DESIGN

Note: Enlarge by 200%

Crewelwork clutch bag

This design is inspired by the detailed and brightly coloured traditional folk embroideries of the Skåne region in the south of Sweden. The finished embroidery has been made up into a simple clutch bag that is the perfect size for your essentials on a night on the town.

KARIN HOLMBERG

MATERIALS

One piece of black medium-thick wool felt fabric approx 27 x 38cm (10⅝ x 15in)

Mora Redgarn 2-ply crewel wool: red (2039), orange-pink (2022), yellow (2002), green (2010), beige (2037), pale green (2009), dark blue (2021), light blue (2017)

Crewel needle size 5–10

Embroidery hoop 25cm (10in) diameter

One piece of medium-weight printed cotton fabric 27 x 40cm (10⅝ x 15¾in) for the lining

34cm (13½in) pink ricrac

Hook-and-loop fastener 2 x 5cm (¾ x 2in)

Sewing thread: black, pink and colour to match lining fabric

SIZE

Finished clutch: approx 24.5 x 16.5cm (9¾ x 6½in)

STITCHES

Backstitch (p. 92)
Cross stitch (p. 94)
Satin stitch (p. 99)
Long and short satin stitch (p. 107)
Cloud filling stitch (p. 137)
Jacobean laidwork (p. 138)

FEATURED TECHNIQUES

- Using a hoop (p. 88)
- Transferring designs (p. 88)
- Crewelwork embroidery (p. 136)

Karin is an embroiderer, textile artist and craft book writer from Stockholm. She likes flowers, retro wallpapers, clothing, haberdashery, birds, folklore, Russian dolls, cute illustrations, tattoos, DIY projects, painted sneakers, Japanese street fashion and textile prints from the 1950s and 1960s. She runs workshops and blogs about her crafting life at karinholmberg.se.

METHOD

{01} Prepare your fabric and threads

Lay the wool felt fabric on your work surface and measure 6cm (2⅜in) down from one short end, marking along the width with a line of pins (this will be the flap), then measure and pin a line 16cm (6¼in) down from the first line of pins (this will be the embroidered area), which leaves the remaining 16cm (6¼in) for the back of the clutch bag.

Transfer the embroidery design (p. 75) onto the middle section of the wool felt fabric, using the pricking method. Place the fabric in the hoop.

{02} Embroider the design

Stitch the embroidery using the thread colour and stitch diagram as your guide. (Mora Redgarn is a Swedish yarn, although any 2-ply crewel wool can be substituted for it.) Note that some flowers and leaves are worked with a mix of two colours in the needle. The order of working is a matter of personal preference, but you could start with the flowers, then complete the leaves and finally work the smaller details, like the stems and the buds. Alternatively, start in one corner and work your way around the design.

{03} Make the bag

Remove the embroidery from the hoop and lay it embroidery facing up onto your work surface. Fold the bottom (back) section up over the embroidered section and pin in place. Using a 1cm (⅜in) seam allowance, machine stitch along each side of the bag, going over the stitching once more for extra strength. Mark 5cm (2in) in from the top edge at each side of the flap and use a plate to draw a curved edge from the marks to the side of the flap; trim off the fabric. Turn the clutch right side out and put aside.

THREAD COLOUR AND STITCH DIAGRAM

Note: Mora Redgarn 2-ply crewel wool has been used, sometimes mixing strand colours in the needle

Stitches
A satin stitch
B long and short satin stitch
C backstitch
D cross stitch
E cloud filling stitch
F Jacobean laidwork

Thread colours
- 2039
- 2039 + 2022
- 2022
- 2002
- 2010
- 2010 + 2037
- 2010 + 2009
- 2009
- 2017 + 2021
- 2017

Take your lining fabric and cut a curved edge at one end to match the flap on the wool felt fabric but 1cm (⅜in) larger. Fold the lining fabric, right sides facing, just as you did for the wool felt fabric, and machine stitch using a 1.3cm (½in) seam allowance this time.

Place the lining inside the clutch. Fold the lining fabric over by 1–1.5cm (⅜–⅝in) at the flap to create a hem, and hand stitch the fabric layers together using black sewing thread, leaving the first and last 1cm (⅜in) open for inserting the ricrac later. Hand stitch the lining and wool fabric together in the side seams to secure the lining in place.

Pin the ricrac close to the edge of the flap, inserting the ends in the openings left in the lining. Machine stitch in place using pink sewing thread. Fold the lining with a double hem over the edge of the back of the clutch. Pin it in place and hand stitch with a sewing thread that matches the lining fabric, taking care to work small, neat stitches.

To add the hook-and-loop fastening, mark the middle of the flap on the underside and a matching point on the bag back. Pin the hook side to the underside of the bag flap and machine stitch in place. Pin and machine stitch the loop side to the bag back.

The central floral motif is worked with long and short satin stitch.

The flap shape has been highlighted with a ricrac trim.

Embroidery Story

I love to draw and doodle in my sketchbook, and sometimes these sketches turn into embroideries. Most of the time I draw the design I have in mind directly onto the fabric without making a proper sketch first, as I like the effect this gives me. I think embroidery should be fun, so I don't like to plan ahead too much, preferring to just start somewhere and see what it turns into.

EMBROIDERY DESIGN

Note: Enlarge by 133%

Retro floral canvaswork cushion

Inspired by the simplicity and minimalism of Scandinavian textiles, this modern needlepoint design is fresh and exciting and nothing like the dark formal florals your grandmother used to stitch. Worked with simple tent stitch in bold colours, it is pure joy to sew. Make up as a cushion, or frame it for a piece of wall art.

MATERIALS

One piece of 14-gauge mono canvas 45.5cm (18in) square

Silk and Ivory tapestry yarn: two skeins each of Sacre Bleu (114), Grasshopper (145), Big Canary (156), Marmalade (216); eight skeins of Apple Martini (155)

Tapestry needle size 22

Scroll frame (optional)

1.5m (1½yd) medium-weight orange linen fabric for cushion

2m (2yd) of 3mm (⅛in) diameter cording

Cushion pad measuring 45.5cm (18in) square

SIZE

Finished cushion: 45.5cm (18in) square

STITCHES

Tent stitch (p. 146)

FEATURED TECHNIQUES

- Frames (p. 87)
- Working from charted designs (p. 6)
- Canvaswork (p. 145)

HEATHER GRAY

Heather's professional experience in textiles and product development, a formal education in design and the guiding hand of a very creative grandmother set her on the path to owning a needlepoint company with uniquely modern designs and materials. She aims to show the world that needlepoint can be fresh and exciting. See for yourself by visiting modernneedleworks.com.

Embroidery Story

My home is a mix of vintage, modern, industrial, primitive, collected – nothing formal or fussy. I found that most of the needlepoint designs available did not fit with my personal style, so I designed and stitched a few needlepoint pieces for my personal use. After I completed several projects, friends and family raved, and so my company, Modern Needleworks, was born.

METHOD

{01} Prepare your fabric

Apply tape to the edges of your cut canvas. To find the centre, fold it in half gently, first one way then the other, folding it just enough to make a subtle bend in the canvas rather than a hard crease. Where the bends meet is the approximate centre. (*Note: If this is your first needlepoint project, you can work with the loose canvas [see p. 146], then, if hooked, you can invest in a scroll frame.*)

{02} Embroider the design

Working from the charts on pp. 152–155, start stitching the flower closest to the middle of your canvas (where your fold lines intersect). Remember that each square on the chart equals one stitch. Work your design in horizontal rows using tent stitch and the thread colours indicated in the chart key. Stitch all of the flowers and details first, then fill in the background.

Once the embroidery is complete, finish off the ends and block the piece as necessary (see p. 147).

{03} Finish the canvas

Once your piece has been blocked, trim around the needlepoint to leave a 6mm–1.3cm (¼–½in) seam allowance. To prevent your canvas from unravelling while you make it up into a cushion, stitch around the piece using zigzag stitch within the seam allowance.

{04} Make the piping

Note: It is very important that the fabric strips used to cover your cording are cut on the bias. This will help the piping curve better around corners. Cut 2.5cm (1in) strips from your orange fabric on the bias and seam several strips together to ensure your strip is long enough to cover the cording length. Fold the long strip of fabric in half and place the cording in between; pin in place. Using your zipper foot and moving the sewing needle all the way to the left side, machine stitch keeping the needle as close to the edge of the cording as possible. The fabric-covered cording has now become piping.

{05} Make the cushion front

The needlepoint is framed in a mitred border. First, cut four strips of orange fabric each measuring 56 x 10cm (22 x 4in). Fold each border strip in half lengthways, and mark the centre with a pin.

Mark the centre of each edge of the needlepoint. Take two of your fabric strips and match up the centre of the border strip and the centre of the needlepoint piece at the top and bottom edges, placing them with right sides together before pinning in place. Machine stitch the top and bottom borders in position, stopping and starting 6mm–1.3cm (¼–½in) from each corner. Repeat to sew the two remaining border strips to the left- and right-hand sides of the needlepoint.

*Fold the cushion front in half diagonally, right sides facing, to make a triangle. This will position the two adjacent border strips on top of each other with right sides facing. Using a ruler and pen, mark the 45-degree seam line for mitring

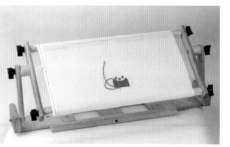

Start stitching in the centre of the fabric.

Embroider the flowers first.

Then fill in the background.

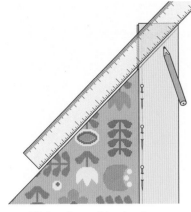

Mitring the cushion borders.

the corner. Make sure the borders are lined up evenly, and pin along the marked line working from the inside edge of the border to the corner. Stitch along the seam line. Begin your first stitch in the last stitch you made when attaching the border to ensure that there is no gap between the border line and the mitre. Open out to check the seam. Re-fold, then trim the excess fabric from the back of the mitred border to leave a 6mm–1.3cm (¼–½in) seam allowance.

Repeat from * to complete the three remaining corners.

{06} Attach the piping

Pin the piping to the cushion front, placing it so that the stitching on the piping is in line with the cushion seam allowance. It's impossible to get a perfect 90-degree corner with piping, so you'll have to settle for a slightly rounded corner: cut a series of small diagonal slits in the piping's seam allowance exactly where the piping will turn the corner to make it as smooth and tight as possible.

Use your zipper foot attachment to machine stitch the pinned piping in place, stitching on top of the seam so you are right up against the rounded part of the piping. When you reach a corner, move slowly and carefully to continue to keep your stitching in line with the stitching of the piping. When you reach the end, where your piping overlaps, again moving slowly and carefully, continue your seam over the two overlapped pieces of piping. Trim off the extra piping from the start and finish so that the ends are in line with the edge of the seam allowance.

{07} Join the front and back

Cut a 45.5cm (18in) square of orange fabric for the cushion back. Place the back on top of the front with right sides together, aligning the edges; pin in place. Again using the zipper foot, machine stitch together on the seam allowance, leaving an opening for turning through. Take extra care when stitching around the corners to keep the stitching smooth and close against the piping. When you go over the overlap at the start and finish of the piping, simply sew right over it as if it were flat.

Trim the fabric at the corners, then turn your cushion cover right side out through the gap, and carefully poke out the corners.

{08} Fill and close the cushion

Insert the cushion pad into the cushion cover and pin the edges together at the opening, folding the seam allowances to the inside. Using a matching thread, slip stitch the opening closed.

Note

Start and stop your piping by letting it overlap in the seam that joins your piping to the front of your cushion. It's best to plan for this overlap to be at the bottom of the cushion. Once you've gone all the way around and reached the start point, leave the remaining piping a few centimetres long and unpinned. The two ends of the piping will overlap and they will need to slope slightly so that they begin to gradually run off the cushion front.

Bargello cuff bracelet

Bargello is a counted thread needlework technique where straight, vertical stitches are repeated following a charted pattern to produce fantastic geometric designs. The pomegranate is a popular Bargello design, maybe because it looks a little bit like hearts, and it is a great decorative motif for this beautiful cuff bracelet.

MATERIALS

One piece of white 28-count evenweave fabric 21.5 x 30.5cm (8½ x 12in)

Cotton perlé No 5: dark lavender (DMC 208), red (DMC 321), dark steel grey (DMC 414), pearl grey (DMC 415), light pale yellow (DMC 745), dark navy blue (DMC 823), antique violet (DMC 3041), light antique violet (DMC 3042)

Silver metallic stranded cotton (floss)

Embroidery needle size 1

Split rail wooden scroll frame

One piece of fabric approx 21.5 x 30.5cm (8½ x 12in) for the backing

Thin interfacing

Invisible sewing thread

Beading elastic and round decorative bead for fastening

SIZE

Finished bracelet: 16.5 x 6.5cm (6½ x 2½in)

Note: The measurement of the finished piece may vary slightly depending on tension used while stitching.

FEATURED TECHNIQUES

• Frames (p. 87)
• Working from charted designs (p. 6)
• Bargello (p. 148)

NICHOLE McVEIGH

Nichole McVeigh is the owner of blu poppy studio, an online shop for handmade jewellery and embroidered cuffs. She started her small business with beaded jewellery designs, and Bargello embroidery is her current passion. She has also launched Embody Your Muse, a site guiding creatives to uncover what they want and how to get it. Discover more at blupoppystudio.com and embodyyourmuse.com.

METHOD

{01} Prepare the fabric and embroider the design

Mark the middle of your embroidery fabric (see p. 89) and place it in the scroll frame ready to begin stitching. The charted design opposite shows the basic pattern, and this will need to be repeated. The cuff bracelet has three full pomegranate motifs with a half motif worked at either side; start your embroidery by counting out from the centre of your fabric and build up the pattern as shown on p. 149, working your way out to either side. (For more advice on the working of the Bargello stitch, see p. 148.) Use the cotton perlé thread as it comes and all six strands of the metallic thread.

The border is worked with a row of vertical Bargello stitch sandwiched between two rows of the same-size Bargello stitch worked horizontally.

{02 Make the bracelet

Remove the embroidery from the frame and trim the top and bottom edges of the fabric by approx 4cm (1½in); do not trim the sides.

Cut a piece of beading elastic 7.5–10cm (3–4in) long, fold in half to form a loop and stitch in place in the middle of the left-hand side of the embroidery with the loop facing towards the centre.

Cut your backing fabric and interfacing slightly larger than the prepared embroidery. Iron the interfacing onto the reverse of the backing fabric. Pin the embroidery to the backing with right sides together, using just one pin at each side and making sure the elastic loop is lying inside the cuff.

Working on the embroidered side, sew the front and back together (by hand or machine) a row or two from the embroidery. Starting at the end opposite the loop, at the top where the inner border begins, stitch around the edge to finish at the bottom of the end where you began, stopping at the inner border. This leaves a gap for turning through. Be sure to reverse stitch at the start and finish and at each corner for extra strength, and reinforce your stitching over the elastic loop.

Cut the seam allowance of the interfaced backing fabric to 1.3–2cm (½–¾in). Trim the embroidered fabric so that it is slightly larger and finish the edges with machine zigzag stitch. Trim the corners, then carefully turn the cuff through to the right side, gently pushing the corners out with a knitting needle. Working from the backing side, and using a pressing cloth, give the cuff a press.

Sew your button directly opposite the fastening loop, approx seven or eight rows in from the edge, using one of the cotton perlé colours. Do make sure that both the elastic and the button are centred so that the cuff will sit evenly on the wrist. Use ladder stitch to sew the turning gap closed. Button up your bracelet and admire your work.

CHARTED DESIGN

Note: Each line on the grid represents a fabric thread. For clarity's sake, the DMC cotton perlé No 5 shades used may not always be true-to-life.

— DMC 208
— DMC 321
— DMC 414
— DMC 415
— DMC 745
— DMC 823
— DMC 3041
— DMC 3042
— Silver metallic stranded cotton (floss) – 3 strands

Embroidery Story

Although I liked to cross stitch as a girl, I lost interest in needlework in my late teens; then, just a few years ago, I came across a photo of a Bargello piece and I was hooked. My first attempt was a cuff that took over 40 hours to complete. Since then I've played with colour and patterns, coming up with some very interesting combinations – it's like painting with thread. Use my colour palette, or get creative and choose your own. I backed my cuff with a luxurious velvet-flocked silk, but cotton would work just as well.

New to embroidery?

This section of the book contains all the step-by-step guidance you need to get started. So thread your needle, choose your fabric and read on – give it a couple of hours and you'll be a practising stitch witch!

Seasoned pro?

If you've already completed a few embroidery projects, use this section to build up your skill base. Jam-packed with hints, tips and techniques, you'll soon be tackling more than the basic stitches – you'll be looping and lacing like the best of them. Why not have a go at silk ribbon embroidery, crewelwork, canvaswork or Bargello?

Techniques

Getting started

Can't wait to get stitching? From choosing fabrics and thread to getting to grips with needles and hoops, you'll find all the essential information you need in this chapter to be able to take up your needle with confidence. You'll learn the best ways to transfer your embroidery design, and neat tips for starting and finishing.

MATERIALS AND EQUIPMENT

There is a vast range of needles, threads and fabrics available to buy – here's what you'll need to complete the projects featured in this book, plus a little bit more.

NEEDLES

Your choice of needle will depend on the fabric and thread you are using. The thickness of the thread determines the size of the needle's eye, and the weave of the fabric determines its point. The needle should be large enough to take the thread without strain and should also glide easily through the fabric.

Crewel or embroidery needles: These have sharp points and large eyes, and are used for most embroidery techniques. Available in sizes 1 to 10.

Tapestry needles: Blunt-ended and large-eyed, these are used mostly for counted work, or canvaswork, and for lacing and whipping threads. Available in sizes 14 to 26.

Chenille needles: These also have sharp points, but they are longer than crewel needles and have larger eyes, making them ideal for working with thicker threads and ribbons. Available in sizes 14 to 26.

Sharps, darners and betweens: General-purpose needles for hand-finishing and tacking. Darners are extra-long needles, while betweens are short and easy to use.

Milliner's (or straw) needles: These are longer than regular embroidery needles, making them ideal for stitches that require wraps, such as bullion stitch roses and French knots.

THREADS

While you'll most often be using stranded cotton (floss) or crewel or tapestry wool for the projects in this book, some of the other most popular thread types are also outlined below.

Stranded cotton (floss): This shiny thread consists of six strands that can be divided or blended with different coloured threads and threaded together in the needle.

Cotton perlé (aka pearl cotton): This high-sheen, twisted mercerised cotton is excellent for textured effects. Normally used as a single strand, it is available in different thicknesses, from No 3 (thick) to No 12 (thin).

Flower thread (aka matt cotton): This has a fine, matt finish which gives a softer edge than stranded cotton or cotton perlé.

Soft embroidery cotton: Thicker than flower thread, this is effective for folk art designs on quite coarse fabric, or for matt effects; it also makes for a good lacing or whipping thread in composite stitches.

Tapestry wool: A lightly twisted 4-ply wool whose strands cannot be separated. Often used for canvaswork.

Crewel wool: This fine, 2-ply yarn can be used singly or in multiple strands, and is used for crewelwork embroidery.

Metallic thread: Available in a wide range of weights or colours, these are very useful to highlight stitches.

FABRICS

Embroidery fabrics can be divided into two main groups: evenweave fabrics and plain weave fabrics. For information about types of canvas, see p. 145.

Evenweave fabrics: These have an equal number of threads in each direction. The exact number of threads per inch is referred to as the 'count'. If your stitches are evenly spaced and of equal size, the higher the fabric count, the more stitches there are to the inch – so higher-count fabrics mean more, and smaller, stitches. Evenweave fabrics are useful for stitches where spacing is crucial, as stitches can be placed by simply counting threads. (See also Counted Cross Stitch, p. 143.)

Plain weave fabrics: This term describes any fabric that is not evenly woven and includes fine and woven cottons, linen and even heavy wools.

Note

Some fabrics are easier to stitch onto if stabilised, and this applies particularly to loosely woven fabrics. A stabiliser is a non-woven fabric applied to the back of the fabric. The design is stitched through both layers and then the stabiliser is removed once the embroidery is completed. Stabilisers can be cutaway, tearaway or washaway.

FRAMES

With most embroidery techniques, it can really help to keep the fabric taut during stitching. By using a frame the fabric will be held at an even tension, so your stitching will be more even. Choose an embroidery frame that is large enough for the design you are stitching to avoid compressing already worked stitches. Here are a few options.

Q-Snaps: These are constructed from hollow plastic tubes that slot together to make variable-sized frames. Half-tubes of plastic are fastened over the fabric to hold it taut.

Scroll (slate) frame: A straight-sided frame, generally used for larger pieces of embroidery. The fabric is stitched to strips of webbing on the scrolling bars, which are then turned to move the fabric or to adjust the tension.

Hoops: These consist of two circles of wood (or plastic), one inside the other, with a tension screw on the outer circle. They are available in a variety of sizes and are lightweight and portable.

OTHER USEFUL EQUIPMENT

Tracing paper: For making a copy of the embroidery design to transfer it to fabric.

Dressmaker's carbon paper and transfer pencils; fine-line pens: To mark indelible design lines onto fabric.

Water-soluble and air-soluble marker pens: To mark removable design lines onto fabric.

Tissue paper and white textile paint: For transferring designs using the pricking method.

Scissors: Small embroidery scissors to cut threads and large dressmaking scissors to cut fabric.

Ruler and tape measure: For accurate measuring.

Thread organiser: To store the threads for the project you are working on; cut threads to your working length, thread and loop through the punched holes, and write the thread numbers above each one for easy access as you work.

Tweezers: Useful for removing stabiliser from your stitching.

Thimbles: Available in plastic, leather and metal, to fit the middle finger of your stitching hand.

Iron and pressing cloth: For perfect finishing.

Needle threader: For easy needle threading.

Sewing machine: For quick project making.

Pins: Choose high-quality steel dressmaker's pins for mark-free fabric, and pins with large heads for blocking canvaswork.

READY TO STITCH

Once you have selected your fabric, thread and needle, you are ready to stitch, but there are still a few techniques to master – from transferring your chosen embroidery design to hooping up your fabric, as well as making those all important starting (and finishing) stitches.

TRANSFERRING DESIGNS

You may need to enlarge the embroidery design (using a photocopier or a scanner) to make it actual size, before transferring it to your fabric using one of the following methods. For each project, the recommended transfer method is given for the fabrics used.

CARBON TRANSFER PAPER METHOD

Lay the fabric on a hard flat surface. Place a piece of carbon or graphite transfer paper, carbon side down, on top of the fabric. Place a photocopy of the embroidery design on top of the carbon transfer paper. Use a metal stylus or dull pencil to draw over the lines on the photocopy to transfer the carbon to the fabric.

Alternatively, use a transfer pencil to go over the reverse of a tracing of the embroidery design; place the paper, transfer-pencil side down, on the right side of the fabric and press, holding the iron perfectly still (to avoid blurring) for a count of 10.

LIGHT-BOX METHOD

Tape the photocopied design to a light-box (or a bright window). Tape your fabric on top of the photocopy. Trace the design onto your fabric using a soft pencil, a fine-line pen or a water-soluble marker, to make an outline that will either be hidden by your stitching, or which is easy to remove once the embroidery is complete. An air-soluble pen is another option but as it will gradually disappear, you will have to keep going over the marks as they start to fade.

TEAR-AWAY STABILISER METHOD

Trace your design onto the stabiliser; pin it onto your fabric. Embroider over the design, then gently tear away the excess stabiliser, using a pair of tweezers to gently pull it from the more delicate parts of the stitching.

PRICKING METHOD

Tape tracing paper to the embroidery design, and trace off the design using a fine-line pen. Lay the tracing onto a piece of scrap cardboard (to protect your work surface), then use a drawing pin or tapestry needle to pierce holes along the design lines, spacing them evenly and fairly close together. Tape the pierced tracing to your fabric and use a very fine pen to go through each hole to mark dots onto the fabric. Remove the tracing paper to reveal your stitching lines.

For a more visible line, connect the dots using a water-soluble pen or white textile paint applied with a firm brush, as Karin Holmberg did through tissue paper to transfer her design onto the dark wool felt fabric she used for the crewelwork clutch bag.

USING A HOOP

Note: Remove hoop at end of stitching session as it can distort the fabric.

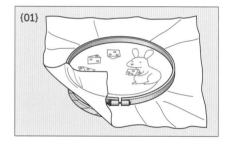

Bind the smaller ring with cloth tape, then place it under the fabric. Place the larger ring over the fabric, centring the image.

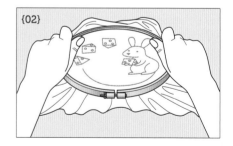

Slightly open the screw on the larger ring and push down. Pull the fabric edges to make sure it is taut, and tighten the screw.

PREPARING FABRIC AND THREADS

If the embroidered fabric is likely to be laundered, it is best to wash, dry and press the fabric before stitching. Specialist embroidery fabric won't need prewashing, but do press it.

Embroidery fabric should be cut at least 5cm (2in) larger all the way around. (But if you want to frame or mount the finished embroidery, allow at least twice that amount.) To prevent fraying, secure the edges of the fabric with a row of zigzag stitches, or cut close to the edge using pinking shears. For embroidery canvas or heavy fabrics, bind the edges with cloth tape or hem the edges.

Finding the centre of the fabric: For regular-shaped fabric, simply fold the fabric twice from edge to edge and mark the middle point.

Drawing guidelines on fabric: While you are practising stitches, it can be useful to draw guidelines onto your fabric first, using a ruler with a graphite pencil or air- or water-soluble pen to mark the guidelines.

Thread length: Generally a good thread length to work with in your needle is approx 50cm (20in), but when working with metallic threads you should use shorter lengths of approx 30cm (12in) as they can become more easily tangled and frayed.

STARTING THREAD

You should never start your stitching with a knot at the back of your first stitch, as this will result in unsightly bumps. For neat results, use one of the following methods.

OVERSTITCHING

Pull threaded needle through the fabric from the back to the front, leaving a tail at the back 4cm (1½in) long. Begin stitching, holding this thread at the back of the work until it is secured by your stitches. Trim off excess thread.

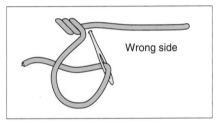

Wrong side

USING A KNOT

Make a knot at the end of the thread and take the needle down on the **front** of the fabric. (Working left to right, position knot 4cm/1½in to right of first stitch.) Work stitches over thread at the back. When secure, cut off the knot and pull the thread tail to the back.

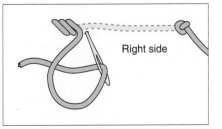

Right side

AWAY WASTE KNOT

Make a knot at end of thread and take the needle down on front of fabric, approx 15cm (6in) away from stitching area. To finish, clip knot and weave the thread tail into back of work.

FINISHING OFF THREAD

Take needle through to back of fabric and weave it in and out of three or four adjacent stitches. Pull the thread through the stitches gently.

Wrong side

Note

To revitalise embroidery and remove remaining transfer markings, soak it for 5 minutes in cool water with mild detergent; rinse well, gently agitating. Roll in clean white towel to remove excess moisture, then place right side down on a dry towel, cover with pressing cloth and gently iron from the back to avoid flattening stitches.

Basic stitches

There are hundreds of stitch variations for you to discover, but all of these rely on your ability to produce the basic stitches described on the opposite page. So before going on to explore the different stitch families (pp. 102–135), start by learning and mastering these 10 simple stitches.

STITCH TECHNIQUES

If you take the time to learn how to work the basic stitches properly, you will find that moving on to the stitch family variations will be so much easier. Here are two simple stitching techniques you'll need to get to grips with when practising the featured stitches.

Note

The stitches included in this book – and there are over 65 in all including the basic stitches featured in this chapter – can be grouped into six different stitch 'families' according to how they are worked, as follows: straight stitches, satin stitches, crossed stitches, knotted stitches, looped stitches and laced stitches.

THE STAB METHOD

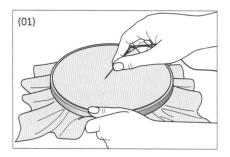

{01}

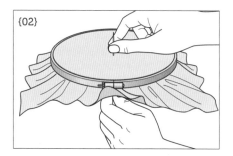

{02}

The stab method helps give your stitching an even tension. Hold the hoop firmly and use a stabbing motion to prick the fabric surface with your needle.

Bring the needle to the back of the fabric, pulling the thread through gently. Then repeat the stabbing motion to come up on the right side of your work as shown in the diagram.

WORKING LOOPED STITCHES

Use your non-stitching thumb to hold and guide the thread around the needle as you work. This will help prevent the thread from tangling or knotting.

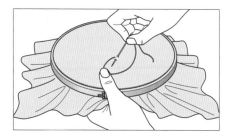

THE POWER OF 10

Get to grips with just 10 simple stitches and you will be surprised at just how varied your embroidery can be. The six card designs featured on pp. 12–17 are a great introduction to the basic stitches you will be learning to perfect in this chapter.

Note

Seeking stitch perfection? The stitch descriptions will provide you with tips for working perfectly neat, even stitches. But once you have mastered the stitches, don't be afraid to bend the rules to explore the interesting effects that can be achieved.

Note

If you are left-handed and have difficulty with any stitch diagrams, place the book in front of a mirror and read the diagrams from the reflection. Often, the easiest solution is to change the direction of working a stitch.

A sweet little backstitch bluebird sits on a stem stitch branch, which is embellished with juicy French knot berries. Backstitch and stem stitch belong to the **straight stitch** family while the French knot belongs to the **knotted stitch** family.

On the beaver card, cross stitch (**crossed stitch** family) is used as an infill stitch on the backstitched tail, while the logs are worked with blanket stitch (**looped stitch** family).

Meandering lines of feather stitch and chain stitch (both **looped stitch** family) make the floating seaweed on the fish card.

The fence detail from the sheep card shows off the herringbone stitch (**crossed stitch** family).

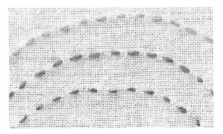

This detail of the water spray from the elephant card shows three lines of running stitch (**straight stitch** family) worked in arching curves.

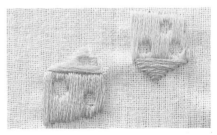

Three-dimensional blocks of cheese spin through the air on the mouse card, created by working satin stitch (**satin stitch** family) in two different shades of yellow.

BACKSTITCH
AKA STITCHING, *POINT DE SABLE*

Backstitch closely resembles a row of machine stitching and can be used when a well-defined outline is required. The appearance you are aiming for is a row of small, evenly sized stitches that imitate a drawn line. Start off by working it in straight lines and then curves to improve your technique.

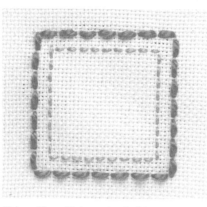

This outline stitch creates bold contours when worked with thread such as cotton perlé (outer), or use delicate flower thread (inner) for a more subtle effect.

Note

Backstitch is an ideal drawing tool. It can be worked over a densely stitched background to follow a motif shape and is often used to edge satin stitch motifs where a gentle gradation is required. Backstitch easily follows curved lines and can be used to create circles and spirals within a design. It is a close relation of double running (Holbein) stitch (p. 104).

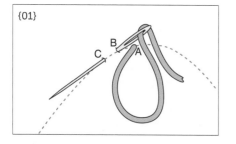

Working from right to left, come up at A, go down at B, then come up at C. Pull thread through.

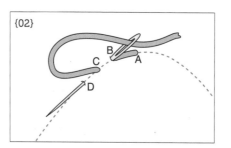

Go down again at B to make a backstitch, then come up at D, ready for the next stitch.

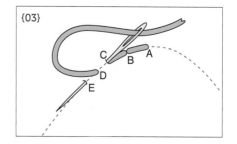

Pull thread through, then go down at C and come up at E. Repeat to work a backstitched line.

Note

You can use backstitch to create a very simple filling that resembles a trellis, stitched with diagonal lines in both directions or, if you prefer, using horizontal and vertical lines. Work several parallel rows of stitches equal distances apart and then work rows in the opposite direction, so that each stitch forms one complete side of a diamond or square.

Even a simple stitch like backstitch can be used to effectively create an embroidered design, like the cabin in the woods hoop picture (p. 8).

RUNNING STITCH

Running stitch takes its name from the action of running the needle and thread in and out of the fabric to create a simple and versatile line stitch. It is worked from right to left, and you are aiming for spaces between each stitch that are equal to the length of the stitches, and for a consistent stitching rhythm. However, when working with delicate or heavy fabrics, consider using a stab stitch method (p. 90).

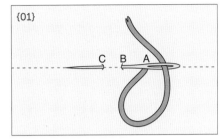

{01}

Come up at A, go down at B, then come up at C. Do not pull thread through fabric.

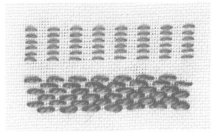

Work this simple stitch in columns (stranded cotton, top) or stagger the rows (cotton perlé, bottom) to add pattern and texture to a design.

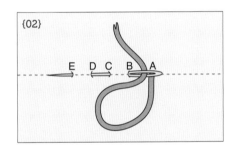

{02}

Go down at D, come up at E. Pull thread through gently, so fabric does not pucker.

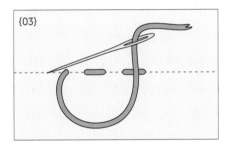

{03}

Continue following design line by repeating steps 1 and 2. Keep stitches even and take only two or three stitches at a time to avoid distorting the weave of the fabric and tangling the thread.

Note

Darning stitch is a long running stitch that can be used as a decorative filling stitch by working rows of alternately spaced stitches close together to form geometric, regular or more randomly spaced patterns. Unlike basic running stitch, for darning stitch it is usual to pick up only a few threads of the fabric between each stitch.

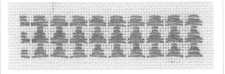

A running stitch border worked with silk ribbon frames the delightful posy design on this table runner (p. 34).

CROSS STITCH

AKA SAMPLER STITCH, BERLIN STITCH,
POINT DE MARQUE

Cross stitch is a simple, effective stitch that can be used for striking geometric designs or worked finely to create delicate pictures. Basic cross stitch can be worked one at a time, or the first half of several stitches can be worked in a row and then crossed on the return journey. Your choice will depend on the complexity of the design. Make sure that all your stitches cross in the same direction and keep stitches the same size.

Adaptable cross stitch can be used for repeating patterns as on the stripe iPhone case (p. 44) or for intricate pictorial designs.

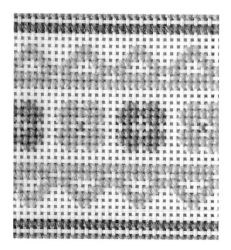

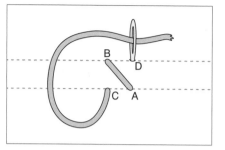

SINGLE CROSS STITCH

Come up at A, down at B, up at C, down at D. The stitch can be reversed so that top half slants from lower right to upper left.

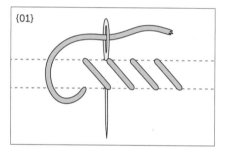

TWO-JOURNEY CROSS STITCH

To work a row, make even, equally spaced diagonal stitches, working from bottom to top. Then go down at top left of previous stitch to work back across row.

Note

Cross stitch is more often worked as a counted thread technique on evenweave fabrics, where the threads between the stitches can be counted to ensure neat, regular rows (see Counted Cross Stitch, p. 143). It can also be a useful filling or line stitch worked on plain weave fabric, but it is important to draw guidelines before you begin (p. 89).

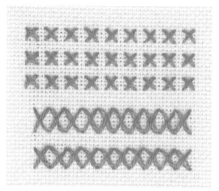

On plain weave fabric, use guidelines for evenly spaced stitches and pull thread through gently, particularly with linked crosses (bottom).

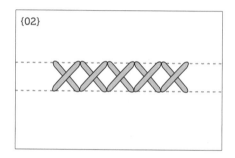

Continue, slanting stitches in the opposite direction to form a line of crosses.

HERRINGBONE STITCH

AKA MOSSOUL STITCH, PERSIAN STITCH, RUSSIAN STITCH, RUSSIAN CROSS STITCH, PLAITED STITCH, CATCH STITCH, WITCH STITCH

Herringbone stitch belongs to the crossed stitch family (p. 111), and is most often used as a border stitch. Draw parallel guidelines on your fabric before you begin to keep the stitching neat and even. You can create effective patterns by varying the position of each row of stitches: for example, the stitches can touch top to bottom, to form a row of diamond shapes, or be interlocked to create a lattice effect.

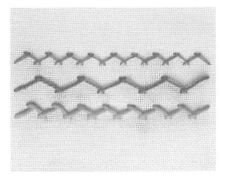

Vary threads and angle of stitch for contrasting effects. Stranded cotton (top), cotton perlé (centre) and matt cotton (bottom) have been used here.

Note

Basic herringbone stitch has a number of variations, but probably most useful is closed herringbone stitch. This filling stitch is worked as basic herringbone, except no space is left between the individual stitches, so that the back of your work consists of two parallel rows of backstitch.

Note

Keep spacing even between stitches, and the rows of stitches uniform in size. Work each stroke of thread precisely slanted. Begin by practising this stitch on an evenweave fabric, then progress to plain weave fabric. When done correctly, the back of your work appears as two parallel rows of running stitch.

{01}

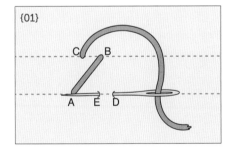

Working from left to right, come up at A, go down at B, come up at C. Cross down and insert at D, coming up at E. Threads will cross at top.

{02}

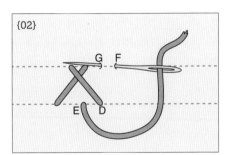

Cross up and insert at F, then come up at G. Pull through. Threads will cross at bottom.

{03}

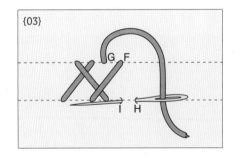

Cross down and insert at H, coming up at I. Continue along row by repeating steps 1 and 2.

STEM STITCH

AKA CREWEL STITCH, STALK STITCH, SOUTH KENSINGTON STITCH

Stem stitch has neatly overlapping lines that give a smooth, slightly raised finish. As its name suggests, it is commonly used to represent the stems of flowers. However, do not underestimate this stitch. It is ideal for following curves and working intricate linear details, and its subtle texture means that it can be successfully used as a filling stitch within a motif.

The stem stitch tendrils on the pincushion (p. 60) are worked with one strand of thread, and the central stems are worked with two strands.

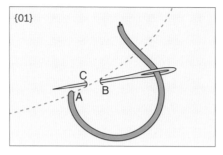

{01}

Come up at A, go down at B, come up at C above working thread. Pull thread through.

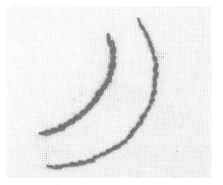

Work this versatile stitch with a matt cotton (inner) for a heavy cord effect. Use a brighter cotton perlé (outer) for textured fillings and elegant outlines.

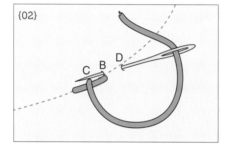

{02}

Keeping working thread under needle, go down at D and come up at B to complete second stitch.

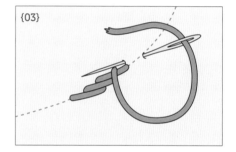

{03}

Repeat step 2 to continue stitching along row as shown, keeping stitches evenly sized.

Note

To work stem stitch correctly, always keep your working thread below your needle. Check that the reverse of your fabric shows a neat row of backstitches; this means that your stitching is accurate. Work with a forward and backward motion and keep all the stitches evenly and equally sized.

CHAIN STITCH
AKA TAMBOUR STITCH, *POINT DE CHAINETTE*

Chain stitch belongs to the looped stitch family (p. 122). It is most often used as an outline stitch, but can also be worked in close rows as a filling. Before beginning, you can define the stitching area by drawing guidelines. Work your design outlines first, and stitch in smooth even rows.

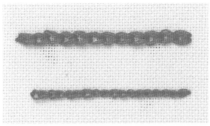

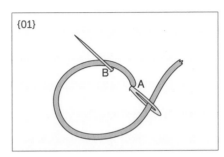

Work as a filling stitch with heavy thread such as matt cotton (top) or aim for an open effect with cotton perlé (bottom).

Note

It is important to keep an even tension so that the chain stitch loops appear consistently open or round. Fine outlines can be created, and curved shapes can be intricately followed. Experiment with lengths of chain worked in single strands of different thread types (see p. 86).

{01}

Come up at A. Go down to left of A, coming up at B. Loop thread under needle point from right to left.

{02}

Pull thread through. Go down to left of B, inserting through loop, and come up at C. Loop thread as in step 1. Aim for an even row of equally sized stitches.

DETACHED CHAIN STITCH

This variation is worked in exactly the same way as basic chain stitch, except that each stitch is finished individually and secured to the fabric with a small straight stitch at the top of the loop. When worked in circles, detached chain stitch is more commonly known as daisy or lazy daisy stitch.

Chain stitch was used to work the brow and nose line of the kitty cat appliqués which decorate each side of the tea cosy (p. 54).

Work a detached chain stitch by following step 1, above left. Pull through and make a small stitch to anchor the loop. Work five detached chain stitches in a circle to create a lazy daisy stitch.

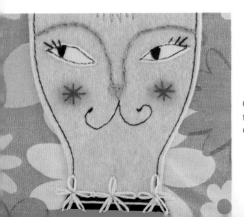

BUTTONHOLE AND BLANKET STITCH

Buttonhole stitches are placed very close together to form a tight line. Blanket stitches are worked the same way, except space is left between each vertical stitch. To work an attractive buttonhole stitch, you are aiming to keep the tops of the stitches level. Before beginning, draw guidelines on your fabric.

Note

Although blanket stitch is usually worked in straight rows, it can also be stitched in full and half circles to create spider web effects and circular motifs as a basis for floral designs.

The breast feathers of the mama owl ornament (p. 39) are worked with scalloped buttonhole stitch.

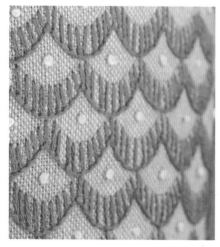

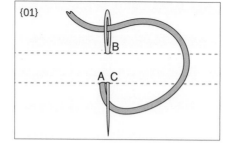

Come up at A, go down at B, come up at C, just to immediate right of A. Carry thread under needle point from left to right. Pull thread through.

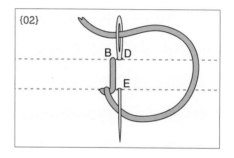

Go down at D (just to immediate right of B). Come up at E, keeping thread under needle point.

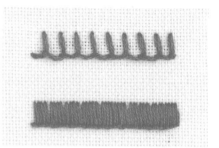

Both blanket stitch (top) and buttonhole stitch (bottom) can be worked with fine or heavy threads.

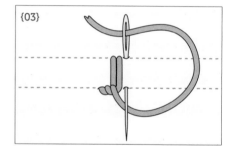

Continue in this way along row, keeping all stitches even and close together as shown.

Note

Primarily a border stitch worked in a neat and even line, buttonhole stitch is perfect for finishing off and giving strength to raw edges. It is an essential stitch for cutwork, an embroidery technique that involves edging a design with a tightly placed border of stitches and cutting away unwanted areas of fabric in between with sharp-pointed scissors to create an openwork effect.

SATIN STITCH

AKA DAMASK STITCH

Satin stitch is made up of simple straight stitches laid close together in parallel lines to create a solid yet smooth filling stitch. It can be used to fill motifs of all shapes, and it is an essential stitch for crewelwork (p. 136). For the best results, stretch your fabric over a frame and place stitches next to each other to prevent the background fabric from showing through.

Note

Begin at the narrowest point of the motif and work from the bottom to the top, taking care to keep the edges smooth and ensuring the threads lie parallel to each other. It helps to outline your motif with backstitch (p. 92) before you work the satin stitch. Place the stitches just over the backstitch line to make sure of an even edge. Draw guidelines on your background fabric before you begin. Avoid making long stitches, as they can become loose and untidy – it is better to split your motif into smaller areas. To fill a large motif, you can use long and short satin stitch (p. 107) as an alternative.

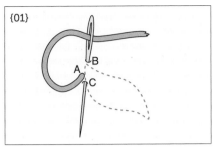

{01}

Come up at A, go down at B, come up at C. Pull thread through gently, ready for next stitch.

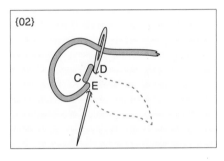

{02}

Placing stitches close together, go down at D and come up at E. Follow exact guidelines of motif for even edge.

RAISED SATIN STITCH

Raised satin stitch is worked over a stitched or padded base to give your motif a three-dimensional effect. Work a bottom layer of stitches in satin stitch and secure the thread. Then work over the base stitches in the opposite direction: come up at W, go down at X, up at Y, and down at Z. Continue until the base stitches are completely covered.

Choose a lustrous thread that will cover the fabric well such as stranded cotton, cotton perlé or silk threads. Using a thicker thread will cover the fabric more quickly.

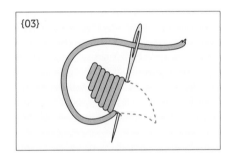

{03}

Continue to fill motif, keeping an even tension so that the surface remains smooth.

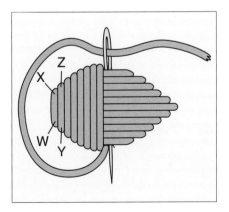

FRENCH KNOT
AKA FRENCH DOT, KNOTTED STITCH, TWISTED KNOT STITCH, WOUND STITCH

The French knot is a compact raised stitch resembling a bead lying on its side. It can be used individually for details such as eyes, or in a row where a soft edge is required. You can achieve stunning results by grouping them close together to create a densely covered area, and they can also be worked in small groups to form a flower centre.

Note

Achieving the perfect French knot requires some practice, and it helps to stretch your fabric over a frame or hoop so that both your hands are free. You can wrap the thread around the needle in a clockwise or anti-clockwise direction, as long as you are consistent. You can increase the knot size by using more strands of thread in the needle, using a heavier thread or increasing the number of wraps. Take extra care with multiple wraps, because the thread is more likely to tangle. If using loose-woven fabric, work over a thread or intersection or the knot will pull through to the back of the fabric.

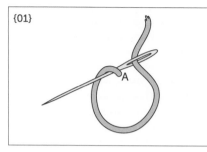

{01}

Come up at A and wrap thread around needle once in anti-clockwise direction.

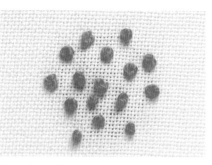

These bead-like stitches are worked here in cotton perlé using two and three wraps of thread.

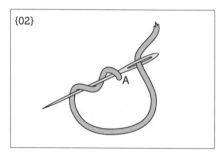

{02}

Wrap thread around needle a second time in same direction, keeping needle away from fabric.

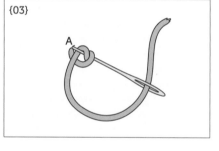

{03}

Push wraps together and slide to end of needle. Go down close to start point, pulling thread through to form knot.

The fleece of this lamb is worked with closely stitched French knots (see p. 15).

FEATHER STITCH
AKA PLUMAGE STITCH, BRIAR STITCH

Feather stitch creates a light feathery line that alternates delicately from side to side. Used as a filling stitch, feather stitch is effective for filling large areas of a motif, such as leaf shapes. Work the stitch in a straight line, extending the loops so that they represent leaf veins. Alternatively, feather stitch can be worked in a single curved line to resemble a fern leaf, which makes it particularly useful for silk ribbon embroidery (p. 139).

Note

Begin by practising the stitch in a column, working from top to bottom. Draw four parallel guidelines on your fabric, and position your stitches so that they are an equal distance away from the centre line. Always make sure that you insert your needle at a downward angle, pointing towards the centre. Feather stitches should be equal in size, and it is also important to keep an even tension so that the loops have a consistent openness or roundness. Once you have mastered the basic technique, you will find that feather stitch works well on curves too.

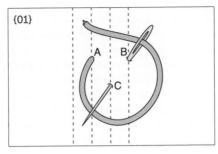

Come up at A, go down at B and come up at C. Carry thread under needle point from left to right.

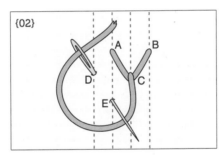

Take needle to left of C, go down at D, and come up at E. Carry thread under needle point from right to left.

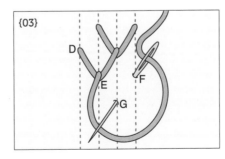

Continue in this way, going down at F, coming up at G. Carry thread under needle point from left to right.

Used for edging and following curves, feather stitch is worked here in stranded cotton (left) and in cotton perlé (right).

Strands of seaweed on the fish greetings card (p. 15) have been worked with feather stitch and chain stitch.

Straight stitches

Straight stitches are the most basic, yet also the most versatile of all the embroidery stitches. If you are a beginner to embroidery, these make the perfect start point. You've already been introduced to stem stitch – now meet seven more of the family.

STRAIGHT STITCH
AKA STROKE STITCH

This most basic of all embroidery stitches can be worked to any length, at any angle and with any thread. When straight stitches are worked closely together, satin stitch (see p. 99) is made.

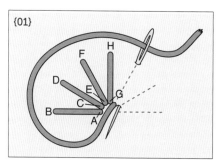

{01}

To create a straight stitch fan, come up at A, go down at B, up at C. Repeat, going down at D, up at E, down at F, up at G, down at H, and continue in this way.

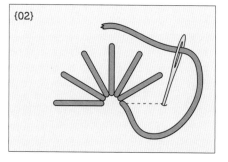

{02}

Once you have worked a half circle of evenly spaced stitches, tie off thread on back of work.

Beginners may find it easier to work on an evenweave fabric, as the threads of the fabric can be counted to map out the stitching.

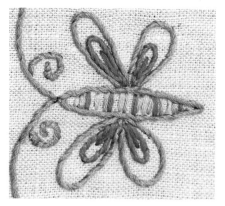

Straight stitch is used for the infill stitch for the body of the butterfly motif as seen on the folk art throw (p. 30).

SPLIT STITCH
AKA KENSINGTON OUTLINE STITCH

Split stitch is similar to stem stitch (p. 96), but here the needle splits the thread of the previous stitch to create a neat line.

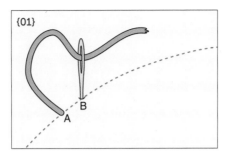

{01}

Come up at A and go down at B, forming a straight stitch on outline of motif. Pull thread through.

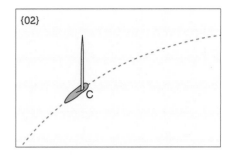

{02}

Come up at C (just short of halfway between A and B), piercing thread of previous stitch as shown.

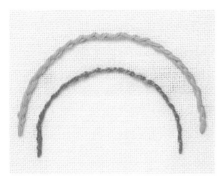

Split stitch makes a great outlining stitch as it curves so beautifully.

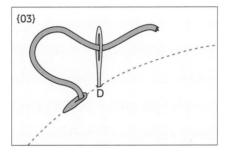

{03}

Pull thread through and go down at D to form next stitch, following outline of motif.

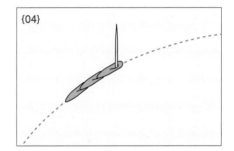

{04}

Repeat steps 2 and 3, continuing to pierce last stitch worked. Pull thread through gently; do not break thread fibres. When row is complete, work a final straight stitch, taking thread to back of fabric, and tie off.

Note

Split stitch can be worked using two colours of thread. Thread your needle with two different colour threads and, when splitting the stitch in step 2, make sure you always keep one colour above the needle and the other below the needle.

The letter V from the alphabet sampler (p. 66) is made from three lines of split stitch worked closely together.

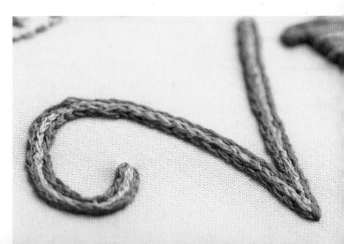

DOUBLE RUNNING STITCH

AKA HOLBEIN STITCH, CHIARA STITCH, TWO-SIDED LINE STITCH, TWO-SIDED STROKE STITCH

This stitch consists of one row of evenly spaced running stitches, with a second pass used to fill the spaces.

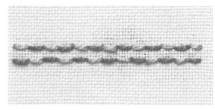

Draw guidelines to help keep your stitches regular.

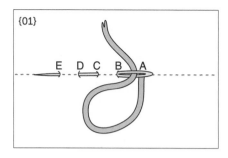
{01}

Come up at A, go down at B, up at C, down at D and up at E. Continue along row, keeping space between stitches same length as stitches.

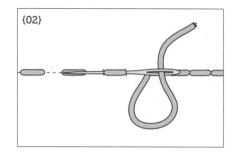
{02}

For return journey, turn fabric 180 degrees. Repeat step 1, but fill in spaces between existing stitches, keeping thread tension even.

Note

Double running stitch is one of the core stitches for blackwork (aka Spanish work) – this is a counted thread technique originally worked as a substitute for lace, where stitching was produced in black thread on white fabric.

ARROWHEAD STITCH

Two straight stitches lying at an angle to each other form the arrowhead shape of this stitch, usually worked in pairs, placed horizontally or vertically.

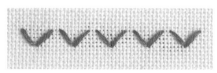

Arrowhead makes a great filling stitch as on the apron of the middle-sized doll on the Russian dolls wall hanging (p. 18).

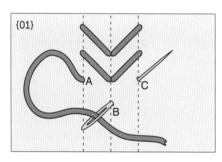
{01}

Come up at A, go down at B (the central point between the two stitches) and come up at C on the right-hand guideline. Pull thread through.

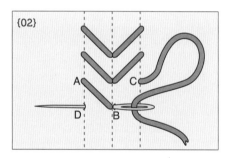
{02}

Go back down at B, then take needle across horizontally and directly below A, ready to begin next stitch at D. Repeat from step 1.

FERN STITCH

Three angled, equal length straight stitches meet at a central base point. Groups of stitches are worked top to bottom to form a fern-leaf shape.

The breast feathers of the baby owl ornament (p. 39) are worked using fern stitch topped with a French knot.

When working fern stitch, draw guidelines before you begin.

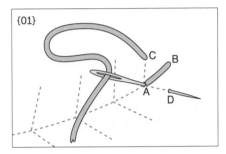

{01}

Come up at A on central stem of design. Go down at B, then come up at C, go back down at A and come up at D as shown.

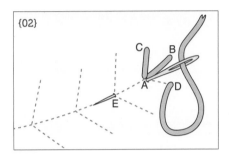

{02}

Go down at A again and up at E on centre guideline, ready for next group of stitches. Repeat from B in step 1.

SEED STITCH
AKA SPECKLING STITCH, SEEDING STITCH

This is a filling stitch consisting of tiny straight stitches, usually of even length, placed randomly at contrasting angles

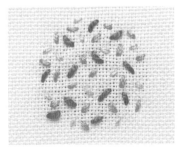

Seed stitch can be used as a light filling within an enclosed outline.

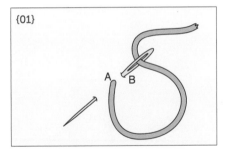

{01}

Come up at A and go down at B. Come up again where you want next stitch to start.

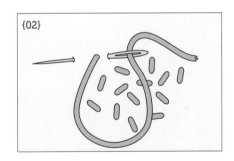

{02}

Work stitches at random angles, as shown here, to fill in design shape or background area.

OPEN FISHBONE STITCH

This straight stitch pattern is worked diagonally and in alternate directions. Stitches are spaced slightly apart, so that the background fabric shows through. Draw guidelines before beginning.

Closely related to open fishbone stitch, fishbone stitch (p. 109) is used for the wing feathers on the mama owl ornament (p. 39).

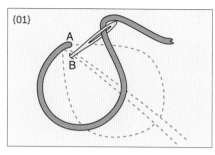

{01}

First come up at A and go down at B, to make a small sloping diagonal stitch. Pull thread through.

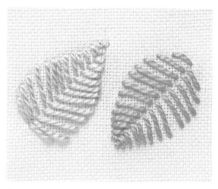

Open fishbone stitch makes a great alternative when stitching leaf shapes.

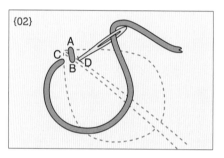

{02}

Come up at C (opposite but slightly below A) and then go down at D. Follow central guidelines precisely.

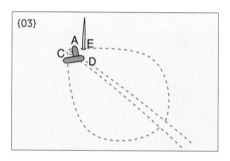

{03}

Come up at E, close to A. Remember to place stitches exactly on motif outline for even edges.

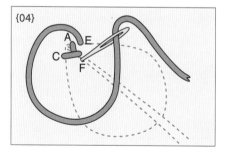

{04}

Go down at F so that stitch lies parallel to A–B, allowing some background fabric to show through.

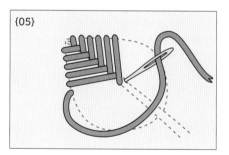

{05}

Work alternate sides to build shape. Stitches should cross each other evenly to give a consistent ridge, or leaf vein.

Satin stitches

Satin stitches are most often used as filling stitches to create a raised solid area in a design. Because they maximise light and shadow, these stitches often give a lustrous sheen. You've already encountered basic satin stitch and raised satin stitch (p. 99); now here are five more satin stitches to widen your repertoire.

LONG AND SHORT SATIN STITCH

This stitch consists of a first row of long and short vertical stitches followed by rows of long stitches. By subtle changes of colour on each row, soft shading effects can be achieved.

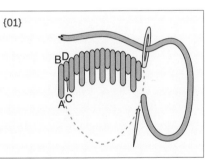

{01}

Come up at A, go down at B, up at C and down at D. Continue alternating long and short stitches across row from left to right. Secure thread.

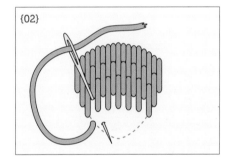

{02}

Repeat, this time working long stitches only across row to fill motif. The last row will require some short stitches.

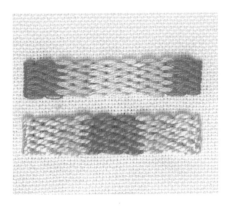

As a smooth finish is normally required, stranded cotton (top) is a good choice, although cotton perlé (bottom) also works well.

Note

Several stitches in the satin stitch family are commonly used for shading, with long and short satin stitch being the most popular. It is often used to fill irregular shapes and is effective on circular motifs where the shading spans out from a central point. In basic satin stitch, shading is created with definite bands of colour. However, encroaching satin stitch (p. 110) forms overlapping rows of stitches, allowing for gradation of colour within a single section of motif.

BASKET FILLING STITCH
AKA BASKET SATIN STITCH

Four horizontal and four vertical straight stitches, all of equal length, are worked in adjacent blocks. This stitch works best on evenweave fabrics.

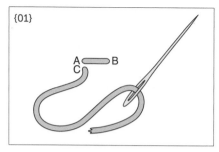

Come up at A, go down at B and up at C as shown to work block of horizontal straight stitches.

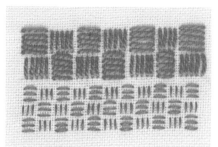

Basket filling stitch makes a very effective infill pattern. The play of light on the alternating blocks makes it appear as if two different colours have been used.

Note

Satin stitches call for smooth surfaces and even edges. Although these stitches are quite simple, success certainly depends upon the careful positioning of each individual stitch. When you are filling a motif, you should pay special attention to graduating the edges gently, as jagged edges can spoil the smooth look you are trying to achieve. It sometimes helps to define the edge of the motif, so experiment with different outlines; try using stitches such as stem stitch (p. 96) or split stitch (p. 103). The texture of linear stitches such as these highlights the solidity and smoothness of the satin stitches.

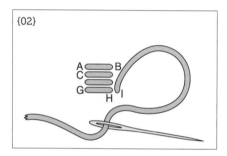

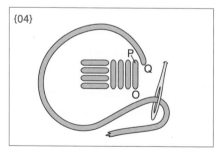

Complete four stitches, coming up at G and going down at H. Come up at I, ready to work next block.

Repeat block, placing stitches vertically: go down at J, up at K and so on. Keep stitches evenly spaced.

Complete four vertical stitches, coming up at O and going down at P. Come up at Q as shown. Repeat block of horizontal stitches. Make sure that stitches are of equal length to keep block shapes regular.

FISHBONE STITCH

Straight stitches are worked diagonally, and these cross over slightly on a central line to form a thin spine.

The stalk of the letter I from the alphabet sampler picture is worked with fishbone stitch, with a lazy daisy flower to top it off.

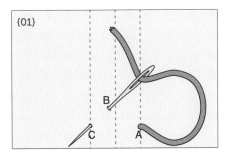

{01}

Bring needle up at A and go down at B, slightly to left of centre guideline. Come up at C.

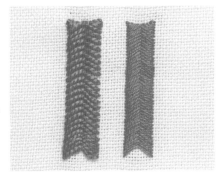

Draw guidelines before beginning to work rows of fishbone stitch.

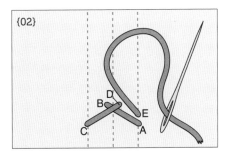

{02}

Go down at D, slightly to right of centre guideline, crossing over stitch A–B and coming up at E.

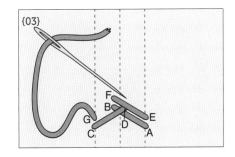

{03}

Go down at F, slightly to left of centre guideline, and come up at G. Pull thread through.

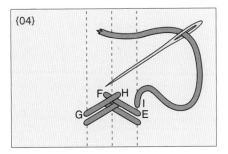

{04}

Go down at H, crossing over stitch E–F, and then come up at I. Pull thread through.

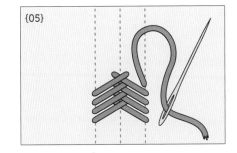

{05}

Continue in this way, overlapping stitches close to central guideline, until column is complete.

RAISED FISHBONE STITCH

This stitch is created by criss-crossing the thread from one side of the motif to the other.

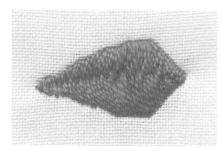

Draw guidelines before beginning to work the raised fishbone stitch.

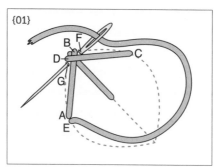

{01}

Make a vertical stitch from centre of motif to tip. Then come up at A, down at B, up at C, down at D, up at E, down at F and up at G.

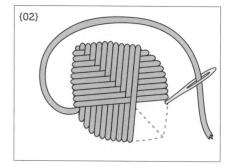

{02}

Continue placing each stitch flush to the one above and following outline until motif is filled. Take care to gently graduate the motif outline.

Note

Both fishbone stitch and raised fishbone stitch can be used to make leaf shapes. Fishbone stitch (p. 109) is worked with diagonal stitches placed flush to each other to fill the motif, but a three-dimensional effect can be created with raised fishbone by overlaying diagonal stitches in criss-cross fashion.

ENCROACHING SATIN STITCH

Horizontal bars of satin stitch are worked evenly, with each row encroaching very slightly into the one above.

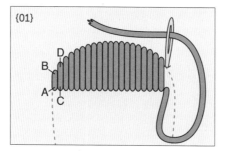

{01}

Working from left to right, come up at A, go down at B (at end of motif), up at C and down at D. Continue to complete row 1.

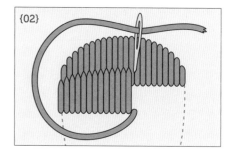

{02}

To work next row of stitches, insert needle between and just above base of two adjacent stitches on previous row. Keep stitches even.

As subtle shading effects can be produced with encroaching satin stitch, it is often used for fine embroidery.

Crossed stitches

Basic cross stitch (p. 94) is an embroiderer's staple, so much so that some of the other and quite frankly more interesting crossed stitches tend to get forgotten. Meet a half dozen of our favourite crossed stitches, several of which make perfect filling stitches, while others can be used for edgings and for sprinkling over plain backgrounds to add texture.

Note

The most basic rule of cross stitch is that all your top stitches should cross in the same direction. If you want to make the most of the crisp geometry of the cross, you should take particular care when spacing your stitches. However, don't be limited by the formal construction of stitches, such as the simple shape of the cross for example. Feel free to experiment with stitches in any way that suits your personal style.

ST GEORGE'S CROSS STITCH

This delicate cross stitch is placed upright on the fabric to form a plus sign. It can be stitched in even rows or scattered randomly.

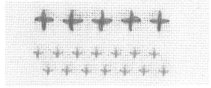

St George's cross stitch is a variation of cross stitch where the stitches are made vertically and horizontally rather than diagonally.

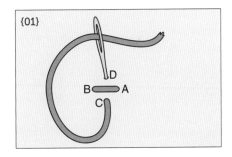

To work a single cross, come up at A, go down at B, come up at C and go down at D as shown.

The 'fat' side of the letter Q (alphabet sampler picture, p. 66) is filled with St George's cross stitch.

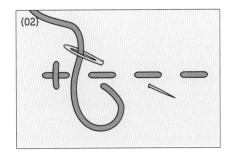

To create a row, work a line of evenly spaced horizontal stitches. Then cross each with a same-sized vertical stitch.

STAR FILLING STITCH

This stitch consists of a St George's cross stitch (p. 111) topped with a diagonal cross stitch of equal size and a small cross stitch worked in the centre.

Star filling stitch can be worked singly, in rows or scattered across an area.

The top row of the polar bear's umbrella (cloud-shaped pillow) is worked with star filling stitch, with rows of bullion stitch roses (p. 117) and loop stitch (p. 122) beneath.

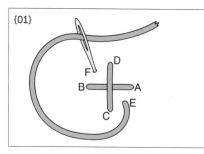

{01}

Work a single St George's cross stitch (step 1, p. 111), stitching from A to B, then from C to D. Come up at E and go down at F, working a diagonal stitch of equal length across middle of first cross.

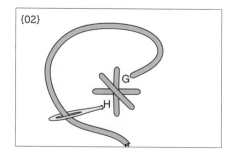

{02}

Come up at G and then go down at H to complete second cross, again keeping stitch equal in length.

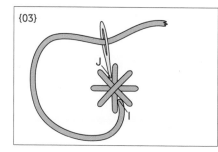

{03}

To begin first half of the small inner cross, come up at I and then go down at J as shown.

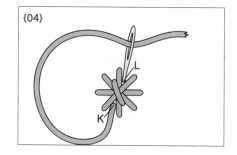

{04}

Come up at K and go down at L to complete small cross, keeping K–L the same length as I–J.

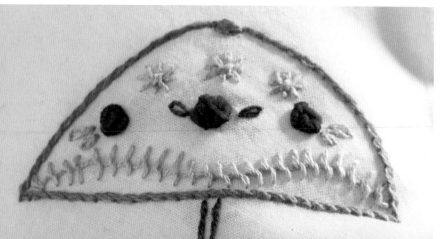

Note

Star filling stitch, like many of the crossed stitches, makes a great stitch for canvaswork. Rows of stitches can be staggered to produce a densely textured interlocking pattern. The key to success is to work all of the stitches of each secton of the design in the same order.

ZIGZAG STITCH

Popular for edgings and fillings, this stitch is made up of alternate upright and diagonal stitches worked in two journeys.

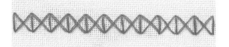

Draw guidelines before beginning and work row 1 from right to left.

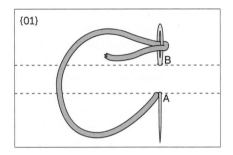

{01}

Come up at A, go down at B, then come back up at A as shown. Pull thread through.

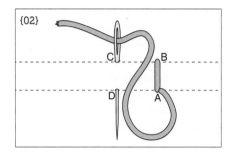

{02}

Go down at C to make diagonal stitch, then come up at D directly below C.

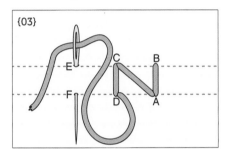

{03}

Repeat steps 1 and 2, keeping thread tension even and working precisely on guidelines for even effect.

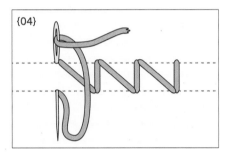

{04}

Continue in this way along row, following guidelines and forming zigzag pattern as shown.

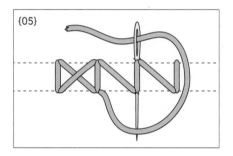

{05}

To work return row, slope diagonal stitches in opposite direction, keeping vertical stitches on back.

LONG-ARMED CROSS STITCH
AKA PLAITED SLAV STITCH, TWIST STITCH

For even results, the long diagonal base stitch should be twice the length of the stitch that crosses it.

Work from left to right, and draw guidelines before you begin stitching.

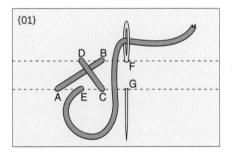

{01}

Work a long diagonal stitch from A to B and then come up at C. Slant over to D and come up at E. Go down at F and come up at G.

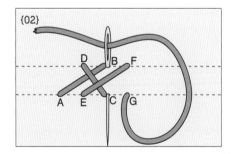

{02}

Cross back to B and come up at C, ready to work next stitch. Continue across row, spacing stitches evenly and following guidelines.

ERMINE STITCH

This filling stitch is a straight vertical stitch with an elongated cross placed just above the base to give its delicate fleur-de-lis appearance.

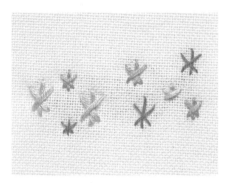

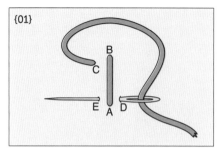

Come up at A, go down at B and come up at C. Go down at D to form central cross and then come up at E, directly in line with D.

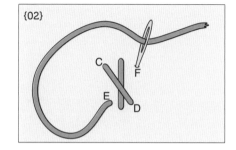

Go down at F to complete elongated cross, keeping E–F the same length as C–D, as shown.

Space the stitches evenly for a dotted effect, or work in rows for a dense texture.

LEAF STITCH
AKA FIR STITCH

The area where threads cross creates a central vein. The length of diagonal stitches is gently graduated, which distinguishes it from open fishbone stitch, worked at a more acute angle.

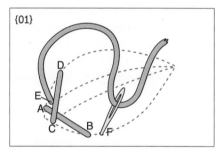

Come up at A, go down at B and come up at C. Go down at D to form central cross and then come up at E, directly in line with A. Go down at F.

Remember that, when working leaf stitch, you are not stitching on a centre line, but to either side of it.

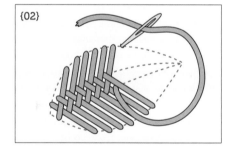

Continue in this way to form a bank of stitches crossed in the centre. Graduate stitch length, and be sure that the spaces between stitches are even.

Note

Stitches in the crossed stitch family can be worked in a variety of different threads. You could, for example, work with anything from metallic to cotton threads or heavy yarns, depending on the boldness of the design.

  Mollie MAKES EMBROIDERY

Knotted stitches

Knotted stitches are a great way to bring texture to your embroidery, so you owe it to yourself to practise more than just the basic French knot (p. 100). Here are a dozen more to choose from. You may find that these stitches are difficult to work at first, but do persevere as the finished results are worth it!

CHINESE KNOT
AKA PEKING KNOT, FORBIDDEN KNOT, BLIND KNOT

This is a close relative of the French knot (p. 100), but it produces a firmer, rounder shape.

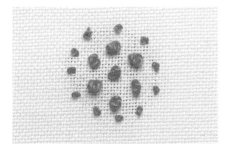

When working individual knots, aim to produce a neat form and regular shape.

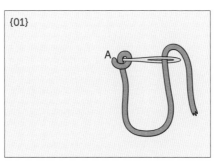

{01}

Come up at A. Make small loop as shown. Insert needle into fabric through centre of loop and pull to form knot.

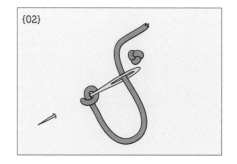

{02}

Come up in position for next stitch and repeat. Secure knots with small stitch on back of fabric.

The backstitch stripes, which decorate the letter O in the alphabet sampler picture, are infilled with Chinese knots.

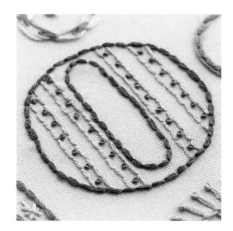

Note

Think of the knots as beads that sit evenly on top of your fabric. Remember that individual knots need to be worked over a thread or intersection, or the knot will pull through to the back of the fabric. The simplest way to achieve perfectly shaped stitches is to work on a frame with the fabric stretched taut (p. 87).

CORAL STITCH

AKA BEADED STITCH, GERMAN KNOT, KNOTTED STITCH, SNAIL TRAIL

Worked from right to left, this is a straight stitch with a knot at the end, good for textured or curved outlines.

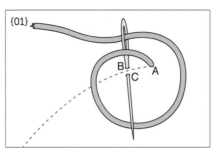

Come up at A and loop thread over needle as shown. Go down at B (under thread) and up at C (over thread). Pull thread through to form knot.

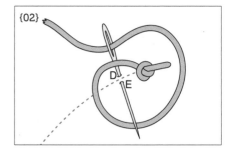

Repeat step 1, going down at D (under thread) and up at E (over thread) as shown, then pull thread through to form second knot.

To use as a filling stitch, stagger position of knots from row to row.

Coral stitch flowers with French knot stamens, worked with 4mm silk ribbon on the table runner posy design (p. 34).

ZIGZAG CORAL STITCH

This stitch is worked in a similar way to coral stitch, with base stitches forming a zigzag pattern.

Draw guidelines if you are working a straight band.

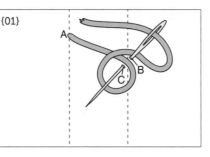

Come up at A, then go down at B above thread. Come up at C, taking thread over, then under, needle. Pull to form knot.

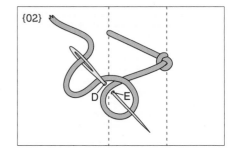

Make a loop with the thread, then go down at D above loop and come up at E through loop. Pull to form knot.

BULLION STITCH
AKA COIL STITCH, WORM STITCH, PORTO RICO ROSE, POST STITCH, GRUB KNOT

In this detached knot, the thread is coiled around itself to give a corded effect. The stitch can either lie flat or curve up from the fabric to add texture and dimension.

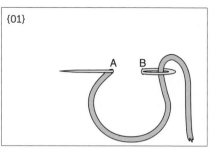

{01}

Come up at A, go down at B and back up at A, as though forming backstitch. Do not pull needle through.

These raised short coils can be scattered for a filling stitch, or grouped together to start to form shapes. The size of the finished bullion stitches can be varied by the placing of your needle in step 1, and by how many times you wind the thread around the needle in step 2 (see folk art throw, p. 30).

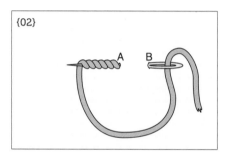

{02}

Wind thread around needle point until a length equal to or greater than the distance between A and B is covered.

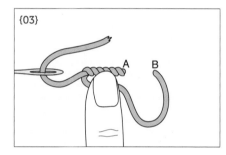

{03}

Hold down coiled threads with finger and pull needle gently through. Be careful not to distort coil by pulling thread too hard.

BULLION STITCH ROSES

Once you have mastered bullion stitch, bullion stitch roses are not difficult to make. Simply wrap the thread around the needle a couple of times more than you normally would with regular bullion stitch to 'curve' the knot. If you do too many wraps, the stitch will not lay flat, so experiment to see how many wraps work best. Use a milliner's needle as it is longer than a regular needle, so you will be more easily able to make the extra wraps. It also has a less bulky 'eye', which makes working this stitch easier.

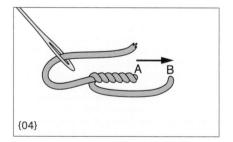

{04}

The stitch now resembles a coiled cord. Bring needle to right to move coil in place between A and B. Pull extra thread through coil to take up slack.

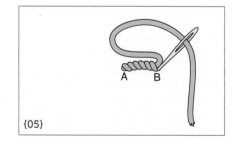

{05}

Go down at B again to anchor stitch in place. If coil is longer than A–B, coil will be raised on fabric surface, giving three-dimensional effect.

When worked in small circles and clusters, bullion stitch can be used to create rose motifs (detail from polar bear design, cloud-shaped pillow, p. 24).

DOUBLE KNOT STITCH

AKA PALESTRINA STITCH, TIED CORAL STITCH, OLD ENGLISH KNOT STITCH, SMYRNA STITCH

The double knot stitch gives a beaded appearance to your embroidery. To emphasise this effect, choose a thread such as cotton perlé.

Note

Whether you are using your knotted stitches to fill a motif or to outline a border, the raised stitches will reflect the light and add dimension to your design; this can complement areas of flat stitching, or be used to accent design motifs.

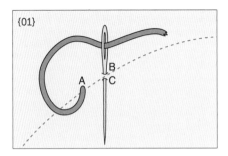

Working from left to right, come up at A, go down at B and come up at C to form horizontal stitch.

Delicately knotted curved lines can be worked to follow a motif outline.

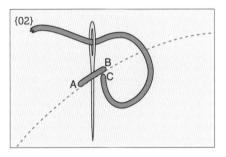

Slide needle through stitch from top without picking up background fabric. You have now formed a wrap.

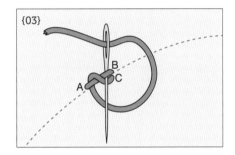

Repeat step 2, sliding needle under stitch and then over first wrap and working thread as shown.

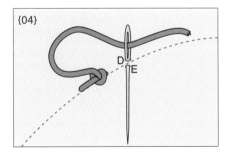

Pull gently to form knot on fabric surface. Then go down at D and come up at E to begin next stitch.

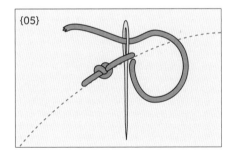

Repeat steps 2–4 and continue along design line as shown, keeping all knots evenly spaced.

Mollie MAKES EMBROIDERY

PEARL STITCH

This knotted straight stitch is used mainly for outlining. It creates a raised beaded line and can be worked in fine or heavy threads.

The distance between knots will depend on the length of the vertical stitches.

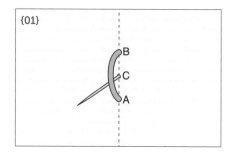

{01}

Come up at A, go down at B and up at C. Pull thread through, leaving stitch A–B loose and working thread above needle.

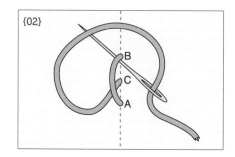

{02}

Make loop. Slide right to left through stitch A–B and under loop just made, without picking up fabric. Pull to form knot. Repeat from B in step 1.

SCROLL STITCH
AKA SINGLE KNOTTED LINE STITCH

Consisting of a simple line of knots, this flowing, wavelike stitch is worked from left to right.

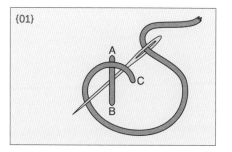

Scroll stitch is a good outlining stitch.

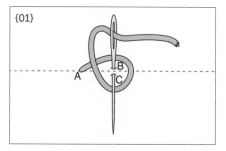

{01}

Come up at A, go down at B and up at C. Loop thread behind top of needle and under needle point.

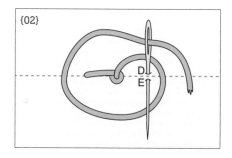

{02}

Pull needle through to form knot. For next stitch, go down at D and up at E, looping thread as shown. Repeat.

FOUR-LEGGED KNOT

This is made from an upright cross with a knot in the centre.

The four-legged knot is commonly used in crewelwork (p. 136).

{01}

Come up at A, down at B and up at C. Lay thread across vertical stitch. Slide needle right to left, under stitch and over working thread.

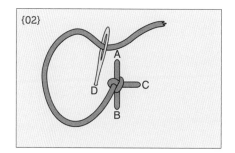

{02}

Pull through gently to form knot. It should be in the centre of vertical thread base. Then go down at D to complete the cross.

PORTUGUESE KNOTTED STEM STITCH

In this stitch the knots are formed by two whipping stitches, to give a knotted rope effect.

This stitch can also be worked as curved lines.

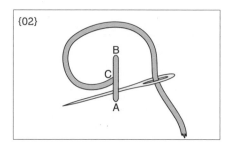

{01}

Come up at A, then go down at B to form vertical stitch. Come up at C (halfway between A–B) to left of vertical stitch.

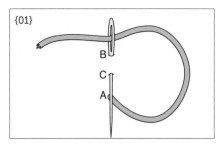

{02}

Take thread around stitch from left to right, then slide needle from right to left under stitch but not through fabric.

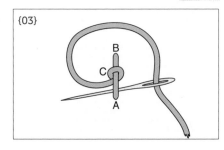

{03}

Repeat step 2, taking thread around and under stitch as before, and pull thread through. You have now wrapped the stitch twice.

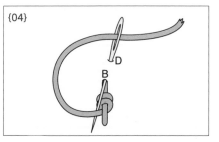

{04}

To form next stitch, go down at D and then come up at B, keeping thread over needle as shown. Pull thread through gently.

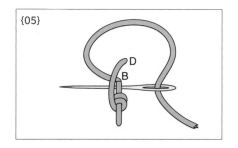

{05}

Slide needle under top half of original vertical stitch and under loop of second stitch. Repeat to form second wrap. Repeat steps 4–5 as required.

KNOTTED BUTTONHOLE STITCH

This fancy buttonhole stitch (p. 98) can be worked in an arc.

For rows of even stitches, draw guidelines on your fabric.

{01}

Come up at A, make loop with thread and hold it in position at top of stitch. Insert needle through loop at B, and come up over working thread at C.

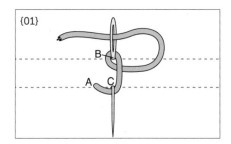

{02}

Pull to form knot at top of stitch. Begin next stitch by making loop, then going down at D and up at E.

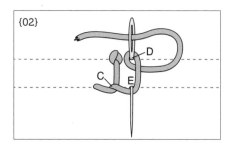

KNOTTED CHAIN STITCH

AKA LINK STITCH

This stitch is made from a chain of knots linked together with a straight stitch. Work from right to left, making each stitch loosely.

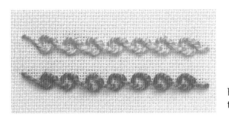

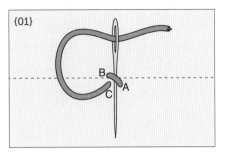

{01}

Come up at A, go down at B and come up at C to form small stitch. Slide needle from top to bottom under this stitch to form loop. Do not pick up background fabric.

{02}

Take thread around left side of loop and insert needle through loop from top to bottom, under top thread and over two bottom threads. Pull gently to leave loop to left. Continue from B in step 1.

Knotted chain stitch is most often used to create a decorative line.

ROSETTE CHAIN STITCH

AKA BEAD EDGING STITCH

Useful for bordering delicate work, this twisted chain resembles braid. When worked in cotton perlé, it creates a raised effect. Work from right to left.

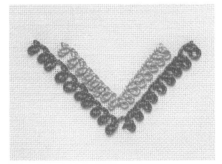

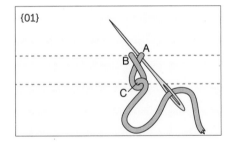

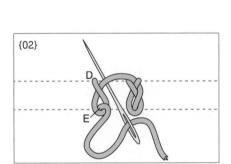

{01}

Come up at A. Make loop and go down at B. Come up at C through loop, and pull through. Slide needle under stitch close to A as shown. Pull through.

{02}

Make loop and go down at D. Come up at E through loop; slide needle under slack thread close to D. Pull to form second knot. Repeat step 2 as required.

Draw guidelines on your fabric for even rows of straight stitches, or work in a circle for a flower motif.

Note

Practise creating evenly sized knots. Most knotted stitches require you to wrap the thread several times around the needle, and you will need to control these wraps with your non-working hand as you ease the needle through to complete the stitch.

Looped stitches

These decorative stitches are used to create braid effects, simple flower shapes and chains of different textures. Circles and spirals can easily be made from many of these stitches – in some cases, they naturally form flower heads and sun or star shapes. They are surprisingly simple to stitch and we have 16 great examples for you to try.

LOOP STITCH

AKA CENTIPEDE STITCH,
KNOTTED LOOP STITCH

This stitch provides a band of straight stitches with a plaited centre. Try graduating the lengths of the straight stitches for interesting results.

Work in straight or curved lines; when used as a filling stitch, work several rows interlocking the 'arms'.

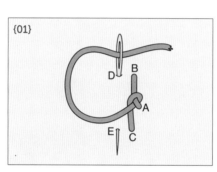

{01}

Come up at A, down at B, up at C. Slide right to left under base of stitch A–B, keeping needle over working thread as you come through. Go down at D, up at E.

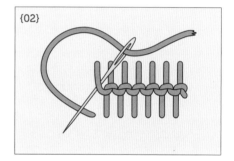

{02}

Pull thread through. Slide top of needle under previous stitch from right to left, keeping needle over working thread, and pull through. Repeat from D in step 1.

Note

Looped stitches are all worked by looping the thread under or over the needle before securing it to the fabric, and the secret of successful looped stitching is to keep all the loops evenly sized. Often, you will find it useful to control the loops by holding them down with your non-stitching thumb as you pull the thread through. Drawing guidelines on your fabric will also help to keep your stitches in even lines.

FLY STITCH
AKA Y STITCH, OPEN LOOP STITCH

Fly stitch consists of a V-shaped loop, tied down with a vertical straight stitch, which can be varied in length. To work vertical rows, draw parallel guidelines and place stitches close together.

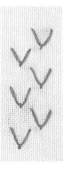

Shown worked in rows, fly stitch can also work well as scattered, single stitches.

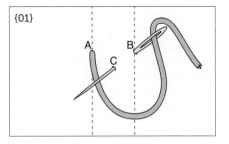

Come up at A, go down at B and come up at C, keeping needle over working thread.

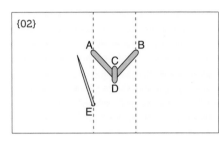

Go down at D, forming a small straight stitch to tie down loop. Come up at E to begin next stitch.

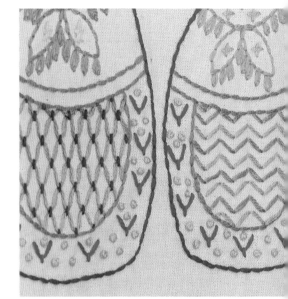

Fly stitch was used to decorate the dresses of the Russian dolls on the wall hanging (p. 18).

TWISTED CHAIN STITCH

This simple variation on basic chain stitch (p. 97) has a textured effect. Hold the chain loop down with your thumb while pulling the working thread through.

The stitches can also be worked separately as well as in a row.

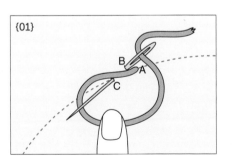

Come up at A, go down at B and up at C, holding thread over and under needle as shown.

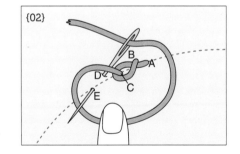

Pull thread through to make twisted chain. For next stitch go down at D, up at E. Repeat as required.

ZIGZAG CHAIN STITCH
AKA VANDYKE CHAIN STITCH

This is used as both a line and filling stitch, and you can work it in a circle to form a flower or star shape. Begin by making a chain loop (p. 97).

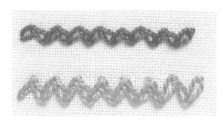

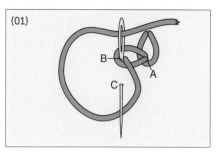

{01}

Come up at A inside first loop. Make second chain loop at an angle; go down next to A. Come up at B, go down next to B and come up at C as shown.

{02}

Continue to work the stitch, linking each chain loop as shown and alternating angle of loops to create regular zigzag effect.

Zigzag chain stitch makes an excellent border stitch.

CHEQUERED CHAIN STITCH
AKA MAGIC CHAIN, MAGIC STITCH

A bi-coloured effect is achieved by using two contrasting thread colours. Alternate the colour by alternating the working thread for each chain loop as shown.

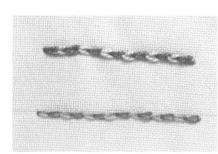

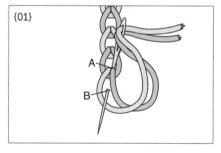

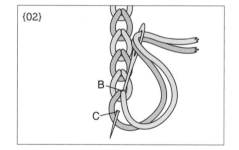

{01}

Come up at A with both threads, make loop, go down next to A and come up at B over one thread. Pull both threads through to form loop with first colour.

{02}

Make loop and go down next to B. Come up at C, keeping needle over second thread. Pull through to form loop with second colour. Repeat from step 1.

Chequered chain stitch is a pretty, decorative variation of chain stitch.

Note

Chain stitch variations work well for both outlining and filling motifs and also provide added texture to a plain chain stitch design.

HEAVY CHAIN STITCH
AKA HEAVY BRAID CHAIN STITCH

This is a heavy line stitch, which is useful for creating a well-defined outline. Heavy chain stitches can be worked in any direction.

Keep thread tension even to work loops evenly.

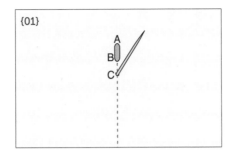

{01}

Come up at A and go down at B to make a small straight stitch at end of line to be worked. Come up at C.

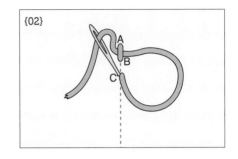

{02}

Slide needle from right to left through small stitch without picking up background fabric. Go down next to C.

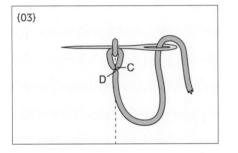

{03}

Come up at D; slide needle through small stitch again. Go down next to D to make two chains in one stitch.

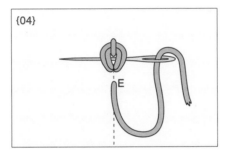

{04}

Come up at E; slide needle right to left through last two chains; go down next to E. Repeat to make second chain.

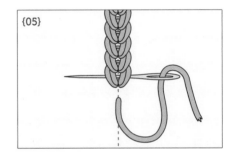

{05}

Repeat from step 4, remembering to slide your needle through two chains at a time.

CABLE CHAIN STITCH

This stitch enables you to make a neatly linked chain with a single movement. Work from top to bottom.

A pretty border stitch that works well in soft embroidery cotton.

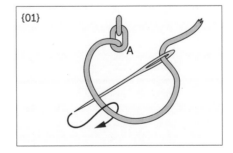

{01}

Make one detached chain stitch (p. 97). Come up at A, then loop working thread over and under needle from left to right as shown.

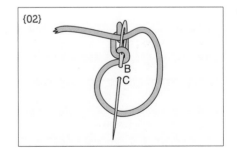

{02}

Go down at B and come up at C, looping working thread under needle point from left to right. Pull through to complete the stitch.

OPEN CHAIN STITCH

AKA LADDER STITCH, ROMAN CHAIN,
SQUARE CHAIN

This is worked from
top to bottom.
Secure the last loop
with a straight stitch
at each corner.

Draw parallel guidelines
on your fabric before
beginning.

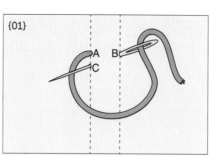

{01}

Come up at A and then go down at B,
looping thread under needle. Come
up at C as shown.

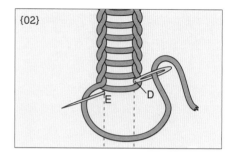

{02}

Go down at D over previous stitch,
coming up at E with thread under
needle point. Repeat to create column.

Note

If you are a beginner, you may find it easier to practise
your looped stitches with cotton perlé as this holds loops
more firmly than softer threads. Generally, looped stitches
can be worked successfully without a frame.

BACKSTITCHED CHAIN STITCH

This stitch makes a firm-textured
line. Vary the effect by using a
contrasting colour or thread type
for the backstitch.

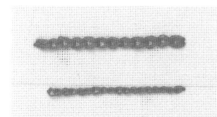

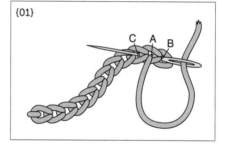

{01}

Work a row of chain stitch (p. 97).
With new thread, come up at A inside
second chain. Backstitch into first
chain at B, then come up inside third
chain at C.

{02}

Continue in this way all along row.
Keep backstitches even, and take care
not to split thread as you bring needle
up through chain.

This stitch is very effective when worked
with two different colour threads.

DOUBLE FEATHER STITCH

AKA DOUBLE CORAL
STITCH, THORN AND BRIAR STITCH

This variation on basic
feather stitch (p. 101) is
used to create a zigzag
of feathery branches.

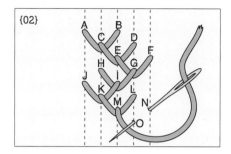

A useful border stitch, double
feather stitch is worked from
top to bottom.

{01}

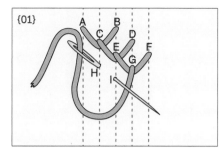

Come up at A, down at B, up at C,
keeping needle over stitch just made.
Repeat, following letter sequence. Then
cross to left; go down at H and up at I.

{02}

Repeat, going down at J, up at K,
down at L, up at M, down at N, up at O.
Continue, working two stitches to left
and two to right, keeping loops even.

WHEATEAR STITCH

When worked in
small columns, this
line stitch looks like
a stalk of grain.

Usually worked in straight
rows, this stitch can also
follow gentle curves.

{01}

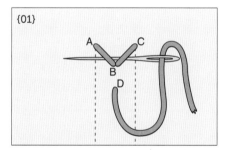

Come up at A, go down at B, up at
C, down at B again, up at D. Without
picking up fabric, slide needle right to
left through bottom of the V-shape
just made.

{02}

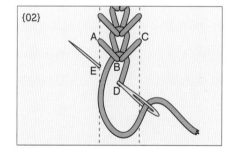

Go down at D and then come up at
E, ready for next stitch. Repeat from
step 1 to continue working column of
stitches as required.

The third row of the cat's umbrella (cloud-
shaped pillow, p. 24) is worked with wheatear
stitch, with rows of ermine stitch and arrowhead
stitch above and whipped running stitch, zigzag
chain stitch and knotted buttonhole stitch below.

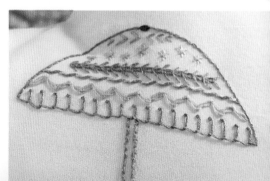

CLOSED BUTTONHOLE STITCH

This pretty border stitch can be worked row above row to form a filling stitch. It is a simple variation of basic buttonhole stitch (p. 98).

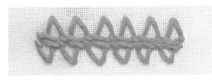

Closed buttonhole stitch makes an ideal stitch for decorative borders.

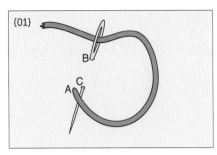

Come up at A, then go down at B and up at C as shown, keeping needle under working thread. Pull the thread through.

Go down next to B; come up at D with needle over working thread. Pull through. Go down at E, up at F, down next to E. Repeat from B in step 1.

CROSSED BUTTONHOLE STITCH

This line stitch features pairs of basic buttonhole stitch (p. 98) worked at an angle so that they cross each other. A trellis filling stitch can be created by working a series of rows.

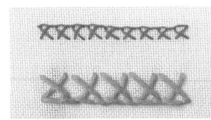

Come up at A, go down at B, up at C. Go down again at A, leaving loop; come up at D through loop. Go down at E and up at F with thread under needle.

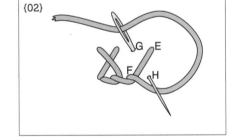

Pull thread through gently. Then loop thread under needle as shown and go down at G, coming up at H. Repeat along row as required.

In this variation of basic buttonhole stitch, the tops of the stitch cross.

PETAL STITCH
AKA PENDANT CHAIN STITCH

This line stitch looks very attractive when worked in circles. The chain loops hang off a rope of stem stitches (p. 96) to create a pendant effect.

Petal stitch detailing on the head scarf of one of the Russian dolls on the wall hanging (p. 18).

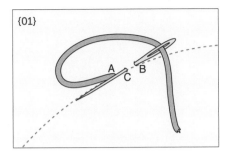

{01}

Come up at A, go down at B and up at C, following guideline and keeping thread to the left as shown.

Petal stitch can also be worked in curves or spirals.

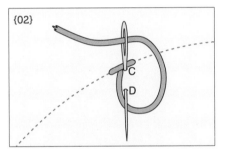

{02}

Pull thread through. Go down next to C and come up at D with working thread under needle to create loop.

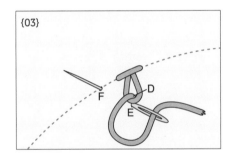

{03}

Pull thread through and go down at E, making a small stitch to secure loop. Come up at F.

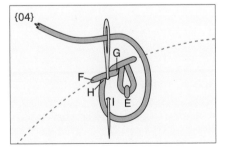

{04}

Go down at G (forming stem stitch); come up at H. Pull through. Go down next to H and up at I as shown.

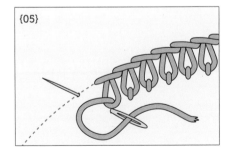

{05}

Repeat from step 3 to form a line of stitches. Work carefully to keep stitching even.

CRETAN STITCH

AKA PERSIAN STITCH, QUILL STITCH

This stitch is particularly useful for filling shapes and creating lines. Work from alternate sides of the shape to fill it.

Draw guidelines on your fabric first.

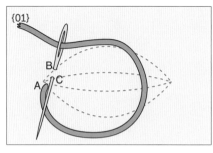

{01}

Come up at A, go down at B and up at C, keeping working thread under needle point.

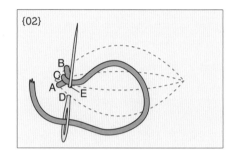

{02}

Go down at D, following motif outline, and come up at E, keeping working thread under needle.

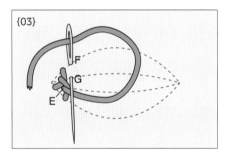

{03}

Go down a short distance along at F, coming up at G with thread under needle point as shown.

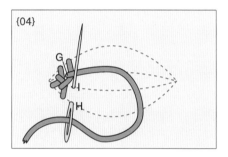

{04}

Go down at H and then come up at I, again keeping thread under needle point as shown.

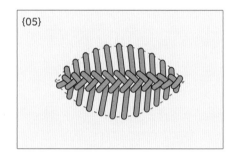

{05}

Continue in this way. Vary size of stitch by extending or shortening the central crossover.

OPEN CRETAN STITCH

This Cretan stitch variation is created by spacing the stitches apart. Always keep the working thread under the needle.

Open Cretan stitch is excellent for following curves.

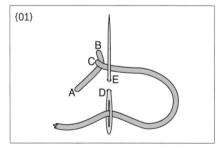

{01}

Come up at A, go down at B and come up just below at C. Cross over to go down at D; come up just above at E, with working thread under needle.

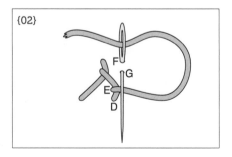

{02}

Continue along the row by going down at F and coming up at G, keeping working thread under needle. Repeat from D in step 1.

Laced stitches

{ *Although laced stitches often appear to be complex arrangements of threads, they are actually made from the most basic stitches, which, once completed, are laced through with a contrasting thread or threads. The eight stitches featured in this section will give you the perfect opportunity to experiment with both colour and texture for decorative effect.*

BASIC TECHNIQUES

The stitches in the laced stitch family are worked using two basic techniques – whipping and weaving. Laced stitches are sometimes referred to as composite stitches as contrasting threads are used to combine two or more different stitches.

Note

When whipping and weaving threads through the base stitches, always use a blunt tapestry needle to avoid picking up the background fabric. Your needle should not pierce the fabric except at the beginning and end of each group of stitches.

WHIPPING

Whipping wraps the thread repeatedly over and under a row or motif made up from a basic stitch, such as whipped satin stitch (p. 132).

WEAVING

Weaving intertwines contrast thread around crossed sections of each stitch to form a pattern, such as threaded detached chain stitch (p. 135).

STARTING AND FINISHING

To start a row of whipping or weaving, come up at one end of the row or section to be worked, using a thread long enough to finish the row or section. To finish, take the thread to the back of the fabric, then tie off. You can choose to work from left to right or right to left.

The alphabet sampler (p. 66) uses lots of laced stitches. The wide stem of the letter R, for example, is worked with threaded herringbone stitch.

Note

Your chosen thread can be anything from the finest silk to ribbon or even string, but the row of base stitches must be strong and supple enough to support the contrasting thread(s). For the best effect, choose threads of equal weight, and always try a practice stitch first.

WHIPPED RUNNING STITCH

AKA CORDONNET STITCH

Whipped running stitch is a neat decorative alternative to plain running stitch and extremely useful for outlining curved motifs.

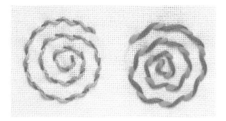

This makes a very attractive twisted braid.

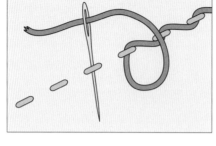

Work a row of running stitch (p. 93). With contrasting thread, whip in and out of each stitch, top to bottom, without picking up background fabric.

DOUBLE WHIPPED RUNNING STITCH

Weave in and out as shown, making rounder loops. For a denser effect, work loops on both sides.

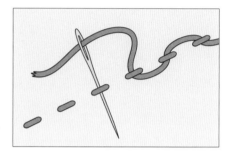

WHIPPED SATIN STITCH

This variation of satin stitch (p. 99) gives an embossed effect and is useful for corded lines, narrow shapes and stems. A satin stitch foundation is worked, then evenly spaced stitches are whipped at angles across the top.

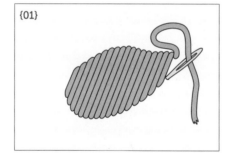

{01}

Fill a shape or work a band with a foundation of satin stitch (p. 99), taking care to graduate edges gently.

{02}

Whip contrasting stitches at a different angle across and under motif, taking care to space stitches evenly.

As with many other whipped stitches, a contrasting thread is whipped over the basic stitch.

WHIPPED CHAIN STITCH

This decorative line stitch is ideal for outlining. The whipped effect can be created using contrasting coloured or textured thread. You can also whip two rows of chain stitch together to create a filling stitch.

Experiment with different thicknesses of thread to explore the effects that can be achieved.

Note
Laced stitches are intended to be ornate so experiment with different threads, textures and colours. A good starting point is to try working all the base or foundation stitches in cotton perlé and all the lacing stitches in stranded cotton.

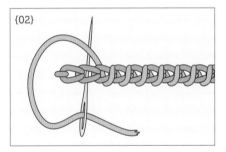

{01}

Work a row of chain stitch (p. 97), making stitches slightly larger than normal. End with a small straight stitch.

{02}

Using contrasting thread, whip needle over and under each stitch as shown. Do not pick up background fabric.

The main vine on the needle book (p. 62) is worked with whipped chain stitch.

WHIPPED STEM STITCH

This very simple stitch is a weightier version of basic stem stitch (p. 96) with the appearance of a fine cord.

Whipped stem stitch follows curved lines easily.

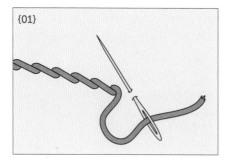

{01}

Work a foundation row of stem stitch (p. 96) with your base thread, following the motif outline.

Note

To use laced stitches to fill an area of a motif, simply work the stitches in rows, making sure that the base of one stitch touches the top of the stitch below and so on.

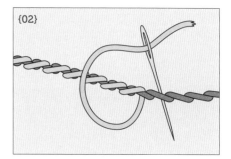

{02}

With a contrasting thread, whip needle over and under each stitch in row. Do not pick up background fabric.

THREADED BACKSTITCH

Useful for outlining, this stitch can be worked in one, two or three colours. Size the backstitches according to the weight of thread to be laced through the row.

Threaded backstitch is a highly decorative stitch that can be worked in a straight line or a circle.

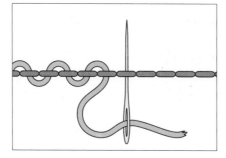

Work row of backstitch (p. 92), making stitches slightly longer than normal. Use contrasting thread to weave in and out.

Threaded backstitch is a very attractive outlining stitch as can be seen on these motifs, which feature on the folk art throw (p. 30).

DOUBLE THREADED BACKSTITCH

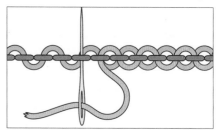

To work double threaded backstitch, weave another contrasting thread in the opposite direction, being careful not to split threads already worked.

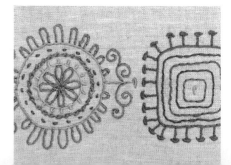

THREADED DETACHED CHAIN STITCH

This easy stitch is made with a row of detached chain stitches (p. 97) spaced evenly apart, then laced with contrasting threads.

The threading loops can be worked in a thicker thread than the foundation detached chain stitch for maximum impact.

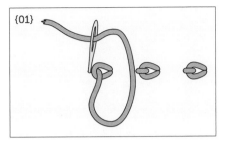

Working from right to left, work a row of evenly spaced detached chain stitches (p. 97) as shown.

The letter J from the alphabet sampler (p. 66) is worked with threaded detached chain stitch using just two different coloured threads.

With contrasting thread, weave up and down through main body of each chain. Repeat in opposite direction.

THREADED HERRINGBONE STITCH

This stitch is made up of a row of herringbone stitches (p. 95) laced with one or two contrasting intertwining threads.

The finished effect is really quite fancy.

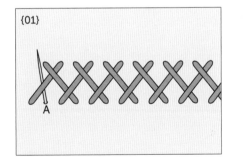

Work a row of herringbone stitch (p. 95) from left to right. Tie off. Using contrasting thread, come up at A.

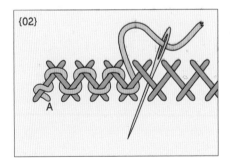

Working from left to right, lace thread under and over row of herringbone stitches as shown.

Crewelwork embroidery

Crewelwork is embroidery stitched with wool, and the fine, 2-ply yarn generally used is known as crewel wool. For beginners, crewelwork offers the perfect opportunity to practise new stitches and to experiment with colour shading. Wool yarn allows you to cover the fabric quickly, and the texture of the thread will hide minor imperfections.

MATERIALS AND EQUIPMENT

As with so many embroidery techniques, success depends on choosing the right threads and fabrics to stitch with and on using the correct needles, so here is a quick guide to your crewelwork essentials.

NEEDLES

Crewel needles sizes 3, 4 and 5: Use size 4 generally, size 3 for working two strands of yarn together and size 5 for very fine work.

Chenille needles sizes 22 and 24: These are ideal for working on tightly woven fabrics such as twill, as they have a thicker shaft.

Tapestry (blunt-ended) needle: This comes in useful for lacing techniques.

THREADS

Crewel wool is a 2-ply, non-divisible, twisted, worsted wool yarn created specifically for traditional crewelwork. It has the advantage of allowing you to stitch with two or more shades in your needle at the same time. As threads have a tendency to tangle and break from repeated pulling through fabric, cut threads to a maximum working length of 30.5cm (12in).

Alternatively you can use tapestry wool, which is thicker (and stronger) than crewel wool, enabling you to cover large areas quickly.

FABRICS

Traditionally, crewelwork is stitched onto a heavyweight, natural-coloured linen, provided it is sturdy enough to support the wool embroidery threads. A densely stitched area is quite heavy, so the weave of the fabric should be firm. You can, however, use any plain or evenweave fabric, including woven wool fabrics, calico and drill, or even a rough, heavyweight silk slub.

Note

Threading wool yarn through a needle can be tricky. First fold the thread around the needle, flatten the fold with your fingers and then slide the needle down over the fold of thread. Alternatively, you may find it easier to use a needle threader.

CREWELWORK STITCHES

Basic shapes are usually worked in a simple outline that is then filled in. Many of the filling stitches used in crewelwork use a couching technique or lay stitches inside a motif to create intricate trellis patterns, and two examples are shown – cloud filling stitch and Jacobean laidwork. They belong to the laced stitch family (p. 131), where contrasting threads are woven through base stitches to create textural effects.

To achieve the delicate wings of the bumblebee (Kindle case, p. 50), two strands of iridescent white metallic thread were used to lace through the small straight stitches, which were worked with one strand of white crewel wool.

CLOUD FILLING STITCH

This stitch is traditionally used to fill crewelwork motifs. It's a great way to fill large areas quickly. A contrasting thread can be used for the lacing to add depth and colour.

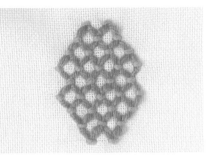

Cloud filling stitch is perfect for filling medium or large areas.

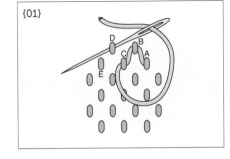

Work rows of small, evenly spaced, vertical stitches. Come up to right of A, carry thread through stitches A and B and across row, going down under E. Don't pick up background fabric.

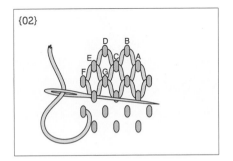

Come up at F, weaving up through E, down through G, up through C and so on. Continue working back and forth across each row.

Note

Crewelwork should be worked with the fabric stretched taut across a frame to minimise puckering of the background fabric and to help keep your stitching even. If the fabric does scrunch up a bit, pin the finished embroidery to an ironing board to make sure it is stretched and straight; place a damp cloth over it and let it dry.

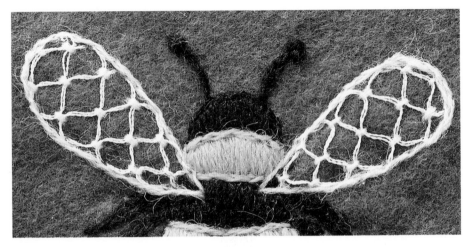

JACOBEAN LAIDWORK
AKA TRELLIS COUCHING

This filling stitch can be worked in a square shape as photographed below, or in a circle or oval, as illustrated here.

Jacobean laidwork looks even more effective when worked with contrasting threads.

Cloud filling stitch and Jacobean laidwork have been used to fill in several of the floral motifs on the clutch bag (p. 71).

{01}

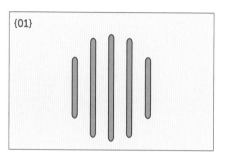

Fill the motif with single, parallel, vertical stitches as shown, working from top to bottom, bottom to top.

{02}

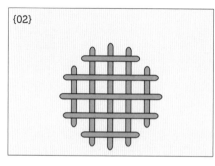

Work long horizontal stitches over the vertical stitches to form a grid. Work from left to right, right to left.

{04}

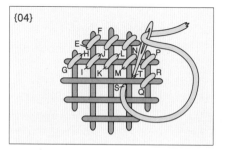

Come up at G, go down at H. Continue back and forth across motif, following letter sequence.

Note

Light, open effects can also be achieved by scattering seed stitches or working selections of crossed or knotted stitches individually within an enclosed area of a design. Many of the stitches described on pp. 102–135 can be placed together in rows to form attractive fillings within crewelwork motifs.

{03}

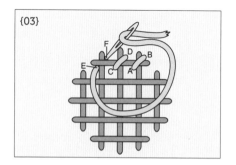

Using a contrasting thread, come up at A, go down at B, up at C, down at D and up at E. Go down at F.

{05}

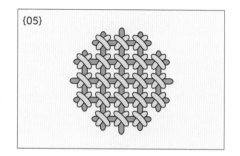

Repeat steps 3 and 4, working diagonal stitches in opposite direction to form crosses, and complete the trellis effect.

Silk ribbon embroidery

Embroidery ribbons can be threaded through needles and stitched directly onto fabric, or folded and stitched with thread to form delicate rosettes and bows. Many freestyle stitches can be effectively worked using silk ribbon instead of threads to give you stunning textural embellishments.

TOOLS AND MATERIALS

Silk ribbon is designed specifically to be used in embroidery. It is available in a very wide range of colours, with standard widths being 2mm, 4mm and 7mm. It is possible to stitch with other types of ribbon, from rich velvets to delicate organza, but do make sure that the ribbons you choose will easily curve and twist into the shapes you require.

Note

Ribbon stitches are more delicate than regular embroidery, so when necessary, wash your ribbon embroidered project by hand with mild detergent.

NEEDLES

The eye of the needle must be large enough to accommodate the ribbon width, and also to create a large enough hole in the fabric so that when delicate, easily frayed silk ribbon is passed through it during stitching, any friction and wear is minimised. Your needle choice will be determined by the fabric you are stitching onto.

FRAMES

When embroidering with silk ribbon, it is extremely important that your background fabric is held taut so the use of a hoop or a frame is essential. It is not advisable to re-hoop while a design is in progress, as previously worked stitches can be flattened or damaged, so it is best to choose a hoop that is large enough to hold the entire design area to be worked.

Silk ribbon embroidered corner motif from the table runner (p. 34). A simple flower is worked with lazy daisy stitch and finished with French knots in the centre.

RIBBONWORK TECHNIQUES

Silk ribbons aren't cheap so it is important to get maximum use from each length. Work with short lengths – around 35.5cm (14in) – and lock the end of the ribbon with the point of the needle to make sure the complete length is used.

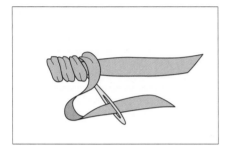

HOW TO START
Make a knot at the ribbon end or leave a tail on the back of the fabric as shown. Hold the tail as you stitch, until stitching secures the tail.

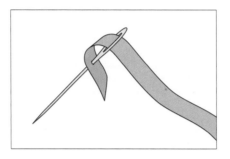

HOW TO LOCK THE RIBBON
Thread needle and insert needle point 6mm (¼in) from ribbon end as shown. Pull long end down, catching ribbon in needle eye.

HOW TO FINISH
Weave the ribbon through a few stitches on the back of the fabric as shown. Or, anchor tail end to another stitch with sewing thread.

STRAIGHT STITCH ROSE

This stitch consists of a Chinese knot (p. 115) surrounded by loosely worked straight stitches. Work anti-clockwise or clockwise, whichever is more comfortable.

The finished motif can be enlarged by adding more rounds of straight stitch.

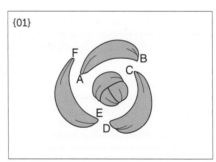

{01}

Make a Chinese knot for the rose centre (p. 115). Come up at A and then go down at B, forming a loose, straight stitch. Repeat, following letter sequence.

{02}

Make another round of straight stitches, spacing them alternately. Stitches can be placed more closely together, depending on ribbon width and desired fullness of rose.

GATHERED ROSETTE

This simple rosette can be applied in layers to make a full-blown rose. You can also vary the shade and width of the ribbon, working the base rosette in the widest ribbon.

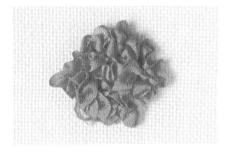

Try working rosettes with two different shades of ribbon for an even prettier effect.

{01}

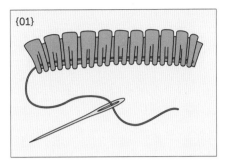

Cut a length of ribbon 7.5–10cm (3–4in) long. Make a row of running stitch (p. 93) along one long edge. Pull gently to gather ribbon as shown.

{02}

Starting in the corner, tack ribbon to fabric to form a spiral. Ends are tucked under. Add more loops in the spiral to make a fuller rosette.

RIBBON STITCH

Ideal for petals and leaves, this is worked by folding ribbon back on itself. The ribbon should lie flat, but do not pull too tightly.

While many silk ribbon stitches can be worked with other types of ribbon, the ribbon stitch only works with silk ribbon.

{01}

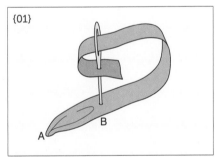

With ribbon locked in needle (see opposite) come up at A and go down at B through ribbon and fabric.

{02}

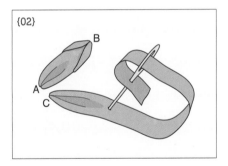

Pull ribbon through loosely and come up at C. Repeat to form a flower head shape.

Note

As you work, you may find that the ribbon length has a tendency to twist. To keep the ribbon sitting flat on the surface of your fabric, use the shank of a pin to straighten out the ribbon as you pull it through the fabric.

SPIDER WEB ROSE

This rose is built on a network of straight stitches worked with embroidery thread.

The finished effect is a pretty little coiled ribbon rose.

Note

Many stitches included in the stitch family chapters are suitable for ribbon embroidery, but they need to be worked with a looser tension than in other embroidery techniques. Practise working some of the knotted and looped stitches in a circular motif to create flower heads. French and Chinese knots, worked individually or in clusters, can produce stunning results. Fly stitch and detached chain stitch are perfect for individual petals.

The posy design on the table runner (p. 34) beautifully illustrates the range of floral effects that can be achieved with silk ribbon embroidery.

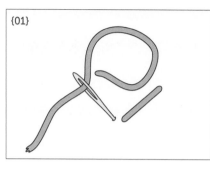

{01}

Work a straight stitch (p. 102) with cotton perlé or stranded cotton. Work four additional straight stitches, radiating from a central point.

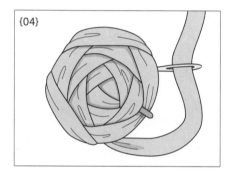

{02}

When web is complete, lock ribbon in needle (p. 140) and come up through fabric at A.

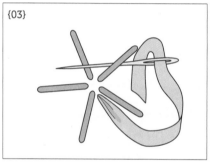

{03}

Weave ribbon over and under straight stitches as shown without entering background fabric.

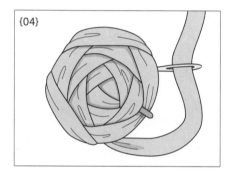

{04}

Continue working outward, keeping ribbons loose until the web is covered. Take needle and ribbon through fabric and tie off.

Counted cross stitch

Cross stitch (p. 94) is popularly worked as a counted thread technique onto evenweave fabrics, where the threads between the stitches are counted to ensure neat, regular rows. A pattern is followed working from a charted design and areas of the fabric are often left unworked as part of the pattern.

THREADS AND FABRICS

Cross stitch can be worked with a variety of threads, but choosing a thread with a smooth texture such as stranded cotton (floss) enhances the crispness of the stitches for the neatest results. It is most often worked on evenweave fabrics on which the threads between the stitches can be counted, thus ensuring neat, regular rows.

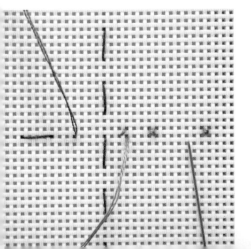

Fabrics used for counted cross stitch are woven so they have the same number of threads or blocks to the inch in both directions. They are available in different counts: the higher the count, the finer the fabric.

AIDA FABRIC
Aida fabric has a clear grid of holes as the threads are woven in blocks, so it is ideal for the beginner to the technique. When stitching on Aida, one block corresponds to one square on the chart and each cross stitch is worked over one block.

EVENWEAVE FABRIC
Evenweave fabrics, like linen for example, have threads woven singly rather than in blocks, and each cross stitch is worked over two threads of the fabric.

Cross stitch can result in very realistic picture designs, such as the bird iPhone case (p. 44).

COUNTED CROSS STITCH TECHNIQUES

There are a few basic techniques you'll need to know to get started, and a few stitches that will come in useful as you explore the wealth of cross stitch designs available to you.

TO FIND THE CENTRE OF YOUR FABRIC

Fold the fabric in half horizontally, then vertically. These fold lines correspond to the arrows marked at the top and side of the charted designs (indicating the chart centre) and will ensure that you work your design centrally on the fabric.

FRACTIONAL AND OUTLINING STITCHES

The designs for the cross stitch iPhone covers use whole cross stitches only, but if you are working on more complex designs that have a more realistic appearance, you may encounter fractional stitches such as three-quarter cross stitch, and you may be required to outline parts of the stitched design for detail or emphasis by backstitching.

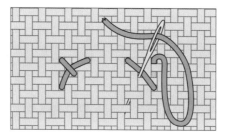

WORKING THREE-QUARTER CROSS STITCH

This fractional stitch comes into its own for adding detail to a design, and enables you to create smoother curved lines than by using just whole cross stitches. On most charts, these fractional stitches will be shown by a triangle within a square. To work three-quarter cross stitch, work a half cross in the direction indicated by the triangle symbol, then add a quarter stitch from the corner over the top of the half cross stitch, into the centre.

AWAY WASTE KNOT START

You should use the away waste knot start (see p. 89) if you are using an odd number of strands to embroider with.

KNOTLESS LOOP START

The knotless loop start can be used when an even number of strands (i.e. 2, 4 or 6) is required for the stitching. For a full description see step 2, p. 46.

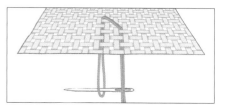

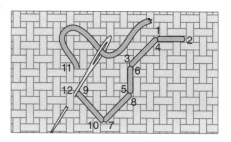

OUTLINING WITH BACKSTITCH

Backstitch can be used to outline shapes, to define coloured areas, to work lettering for personalised designs and to represent detail. Generally, one strand of stranded cotton (floss) is used. Work all the cross stitch before adding the backstitch, and work the backstitch over individual blocks on Aida or over pairs of threads on evenweave (as shown above), bringing the needle up at 1, down at 2, up at 3, down at 4 and so on.

Canvaswork

Canvaswork, or needlepoint as it is often called, is a counted thread technique worked onto a woven canvas of an even count using wool, cotton or silk threads. It is perfectly compatible to the clean lines of contemporary designs such as the retro floral canvaswork cushion (p. 76).

THREADS AND FABRICS

Canvas is used for canvaswork embroidery. The mesh size or gauge of canvas is determined by the number of threads to the inch, and the larger the number, the finer the canvas. The mesh is completely covered by the stitching thread or yarn: choose thicker threads such as tapestry wool for canvas with a lower mesh count, and finer threads such as cotton perlé for canvas with a higher mesh count.

Note

Canvas fabric is usually bought by the metre (yard). It is treated with size to make it rigid. Unlike soft cross stitch or embroidery fabric, using a hoop on canvas will make a firm crease that will be hard or impossible to remove, so always use a scroll (slate) frame.

CANVAS CHOICES

There are various different types of canvas available as described below, and you should always choose a good-quality canvas that is knot-free, with smooth threads that will not snag your stitches.

Mono canvas (aka plain single canvas): The mesh is woven in single threads in each direction and is available in the largest range of sizes. Available in gauges 10 to 22.

Double canvas (aka Penelope canvas): The mesh is woven in pairs of threads in each direction. Available in gauges 7 to 10.

Rug canvas: This has an interlocked construction. Available in gauges of 3 to 6 threads.

Plastic canvas: A medium-gauge mesh, bought by the sheet, for making 3D projects such as little decorative boxes.

The retro floral canvaswork cushion is designed to be worked on a 14-mesh mono canvas, but it could be worked on any mesh size canvas you like. With a stitch count of 168 x 168 stitches, the design works up to 30.5cm (12in) square on 14-mesh canvas, but stitched onto 10-mesh canvas it would measure approx 42.5cm (16¾in) square, and on 18-mesh canvas 23.5cm (9¼in) square.

STITCHING TECHNIQUES

There are many needlepoint stitches, and rich patterns and textures can be achieved by mixing them on the same piece; however, for the beginner to the technique, the simplicity of tent stitch is hard to beat.

CUT AND PREPARE YOUR CANVAS

Allow for a 5–7.5cm (2–3in) margin all the way around the edge of your stitched design. This will give you plenty of extra working space for finishing, even allowing for starting the design a little off centre. Run masking tape along the edges of the cut canvas to avoid catching the yarn as you stitch, and decide if you are going to use a frame.

WORKING WITHOUT A FRAME

Most beginners start off 'free stitching', which is working on an unframed canvas as shown left. This makes for very portable stitching but your finished stitching will require blocking as described opposite.

WORKING WITH A FRAME

Although it is possible to use a circular embroidery hoop, canvas is very stiff, making it difficult to place in the hoop. If you do attempt to use a hoop, it should be larger than your design, as the hoop must not crease the canvas in an area that has been or will be stitched. In fact, your best option is to use a scroll frame, shown opposite, as it will keep your canvas very taut without the risk of marking the stitched area. Frames with stands or supports allow you to work with both hands free, one above and one below the frame.

TENT STITCH
AKA CONTINENTAL STITCH

This stitch gives excellent coverage across the canvas. You are likely to achieve better stitching results when working a design like the retro floral canvaswork cushion (p. 76) if you use a scroll frame.

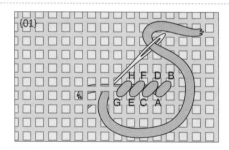

Leave a few centimetres of loose thread at the back of your canvas. Working right to left, bring the needle up at A and down at B, up again at C and down at D, up at E and down at F, up at G and down at H, taking care to work the stitches over the loose thread to secure it.

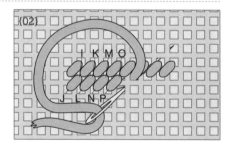

Work the next row from left to right, bringing the needle up at I and down at J, and continuing along the row following the letter sequence shown.

CHANGING THREAD COLOURS

When you need to change colour or you have used up the length of yarn you are using and need to re-thread your needle, you will need to secure the end of your thread. When you have completed the last stitch, with the needle on the back (wrong) side of the canvas, weave (or bury) it through the back of four or five stitches. This will take the thread under the stitches and it will be secure. Cut the thread close to where the needle emerges.

BLOCKING FINISHED STITCHING

When working tent stitch, all of your stitching is going in the same direction, which causes the canvas to become distorted, so although you started with a square, your completed needlepoint will look more like a parallelogram. Blocking is a process of wetting and stretching the completed piece to bring it back to square.

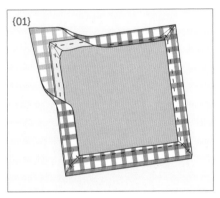

{01}

To make a blocking board, cover a soft board with a layer of wadding and a top layer of cotton fabric – gingham makes a good choice as it provides you with a grid. Stretch and staple the wadding and cloth to the board, mitring the corners.

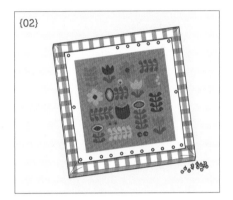

{02}

Dampen the surface of the canvas using a spray bottle filled with warm water. Let the water soak in for a few minutes, then gently pull at the corners and sides to start the re-shaping process. Lay the canvas right side up on the blocking board; ease and stretch its edges and secure with drawing pins. Work from centre edge to each corner, using the gingham as a guide to squaring the canvas.

{03} Let the canvas dry for a few days before removing the pins. If the canvas is very badly distorted, it may be necessary to repeat the process.

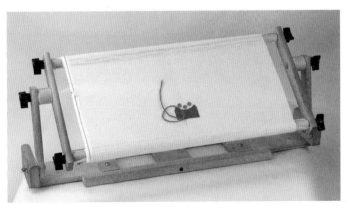

When you work on a scroll frame, the project is held with even tension resulting in a less distorted project, and making the blocking process much easier.

Bargello

Bargello (aka flame stitch, Florentine stitch or Hungarian point) is worked traditionally on canvas using wool yarn, making it perfect for pieces that require durability, such as cushions and rugs. Recognisable by its characteristic upright stitches, it is worked in geometric patterns over two or more threads.

BARGELLO STITCH

Bargello stitches can be worked in blocks of variable stitches, but the stepping is generally separated by two threads (or halfway down the preceding stitch) to create the typical undulating pattern.

Bring the needle up at A, go down at B (counting over four threads of the fabric), up at C, down at D. Continue to complete the first block of 4 sts.

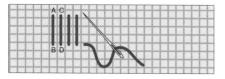

To work the next block (3 sts in this example), start stitching two threads above the first block.

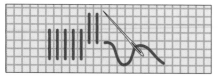

ZIGZAG PATTERN

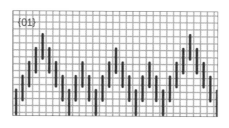

Work a base row of Bargello stitch, remembering to step up by two threads each stitch.

Continue to work rows above, changing the colour of the thread being used each time. →

Step up two threads to complete the final block.

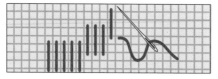

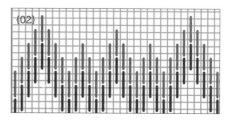

Following the pattern established by the first row, work a second row above in a different coloured thread.

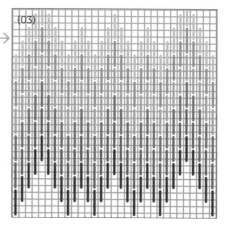

POMEGRANATE PATTERN

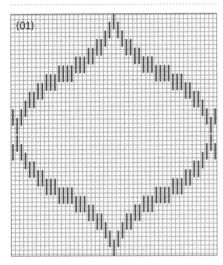

{01}

Start by working the outline shape of the pomegranate motifs carefully following the line chart on p. 83.

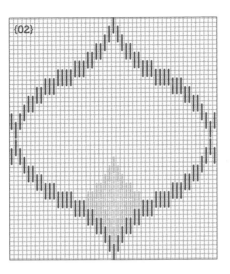

{02}

Now begin to fill in the pomegranate motif working from the base to the top of the design.

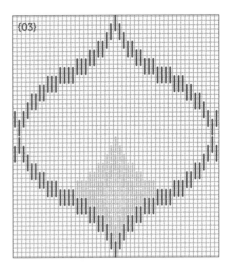

{03}

Blocks of the Bargello stitch are worked over four threads in steps of two, although the number of stitches in a block will vary.

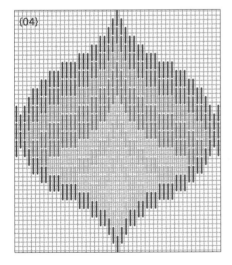

{04}

As more rows of the charted design are worked, the pattern appears to ripple before your eyes.

{05}

Once the pomegranate motifs have been filled you can begin to fill in the background, working from the bottom to the top.

Since Bargello stitches are all made to the same length, you will find that it is quite easy to get into a flow once you have the hang of it. The embroidery can be done on different types of fabric and canvases, as long as they have an even weave.

Free-motion machine embroidery

Machine embroidery is quick and fun to do. Even if your machine only has basic straight and zigzag stitches, you can achieve some truly amazing results with free-motion machine embroidery. With practice you can 'draw' details with the needle, colour in or layer areas, for truly unique pieces.

PREPARING YOUR MACHINE

When machine sewing, the fabric is normally passed under the machine needle in one direction, but by dropping the feed dogs – the little 'teeth' that come up into the needle plate as you sew to pull the fabric through – or by using a raised needle plate, you put yourself firmly in control. For best results, sharp machine needles are a must.

Note
Bind the inner or outer ring of the hoop with masking tape or bias binding to help keep fine fabrics taut. Make sure the inner hoop is slightly lower than the outer ring to ensure good, flat contact with the machine.

DISENGAGE YOUR FEED DOGS

To prepare a standard sewing machine for free-motion machine embroidery, remove the presser foot and lower your feed dogs; some machines come with a raised needle plate allowing you to simply cover the feed dogs, as shown above; either way your machine's manual will tell you what to do. Dropping or covering the feed dogs eliminates the machine's grip on the fabric, so placing you in full control of the movement of the fabric.

SET UP YOUR FABRIC IN A HOOP

To make free-motion embroidery easier, it is necessary to first fit your fabric into an embroidery hoop and a wooden one works well. Stretch your fabric taut in the outer hoop and push the inner hoop down on top. Make the inner hoop slightly lower than the outer ring to ensure the fabric is really flat on the surface of the machine, then tighten the screw on the side of the hoop.

GET READY TO STITCH

{01}

Set the stitch length at zero and place the hoop in position on the machine, taking care that the needle is in its highest position so that the hoop can be put in without damaging or bending the needle. Lower the foot lever, even though you have removed the foot.

{02}

Put the needle into the fabric and pull the lower thread to the surface of the fabric to give you two strands of cotton on the hoop. You are now ready to stitch.

{03} Gently hold the two strands of cotton with slack, as this just helps a bit with the first couple of stitches; you can trim these as soon as you get going. Do a few backward and forward stitches to start off with. Start slowly to get the feel of the machine and to see how fast you need to move the fabric.

STITCHING TECHNIQUE

Hold the hoop firmly as you stitch and experiment with your stitching speed, aiming to keep it steady and controlled.

You will soon start to get a feel for co-ordinating the stitching and holding the hoop down flat. Practise to gain control of your machine and build confidence. You are aiming for a smooth and steady movement, so try to avoid jerking or moving the hoop too quickly. Do not stitch too close to the hoop as the needle will break if it hits it, and do be particularly careful not to let your fingers stray too near the needle.

EXPLORING TECHNIQUES

Once you have become confident with the basics you can experiment with all sorts of techniques and textures from filling in areas to outlining.

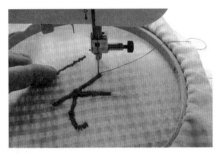
Monogramming with zigzag stitch.

Outlining an appliqué motif.

Filling in (or colouring) with texture.

RETRO FLORAL CHART (TOP LEFT)

Note: Silk and Ivory tapestry yarn used

Sacre Bleu 114
Grasshopper 145
Apple Martini 155
Big Canary 156
Marmalade 216

Mollie MAKES EMBROIDERY

RETRO FLORAL CHART (TOP RIGHT)

Sacre Bleu 114   Apple Martini 155   Marmalade 216

Grasshopper 145   Big Canary 156

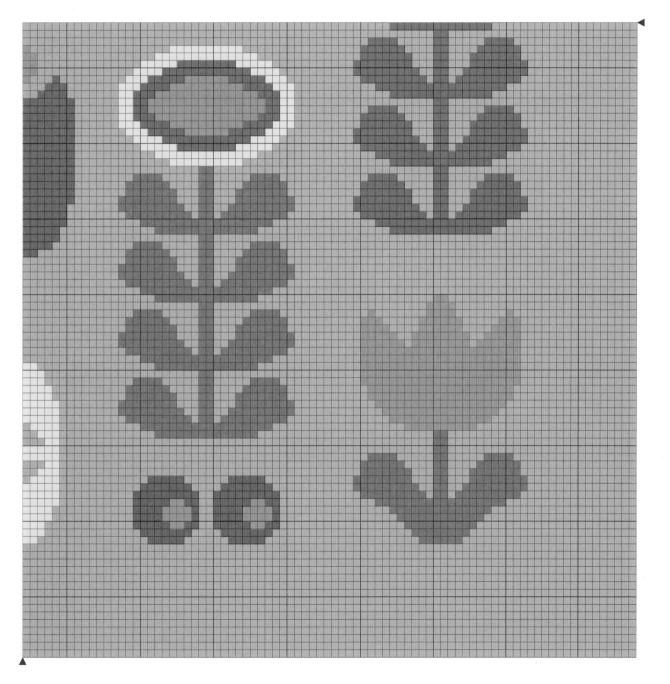

TEMPLATES YOU CAN ALSO FIND THE FULL-SIZE TEMPLATES READY TO DOWNLOAD FROM WWW.PAVILIONCRAFT.CO.UK

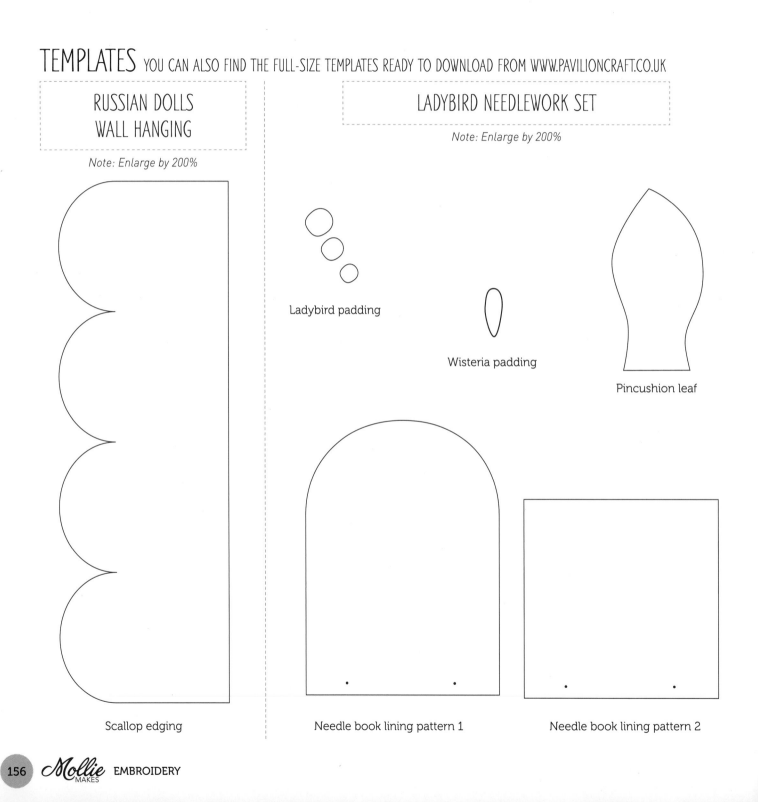

RUSSIAN DOLLS WALL HANGING

Note: Enlarge by 200%

Scallop edging

LADYBIRD NEEDLEWORK SET

Note: Enlarge by 200%

Ladybird padding

Wisteria padding

Pincushion leaf

Needle book lining pattern 1

Needle book lining pattern 2

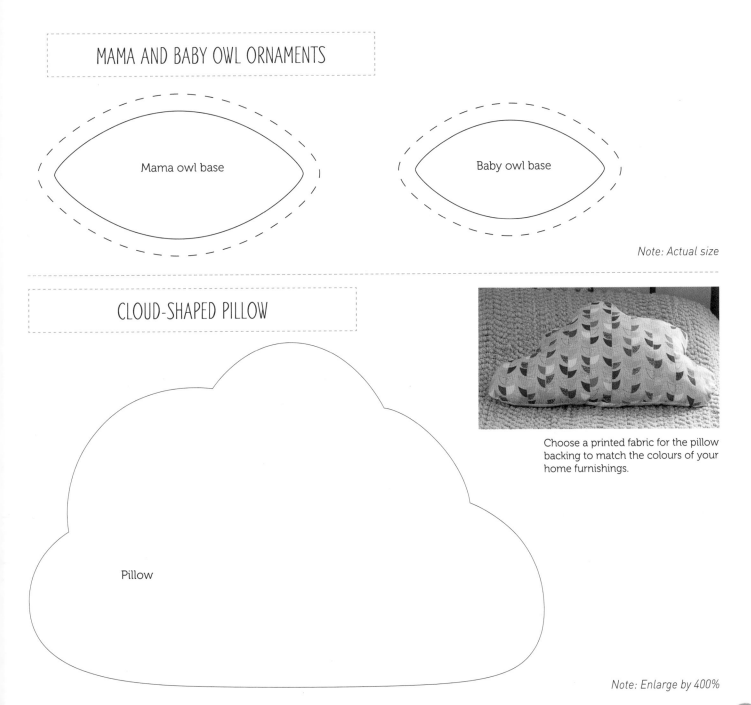

MAMA AND BABY OWL ORNAMENTS

Mama owl base

Baby owl base

Note: Actual size

CLOUD-SHAPED PILLOW

Pillow

Choose a printed fabric for the pillow backing to match the colours of your home furnishings.

Note: Enlarge by 400%

KITTY CATS TEA COSY

Note: Enlarge by 200%

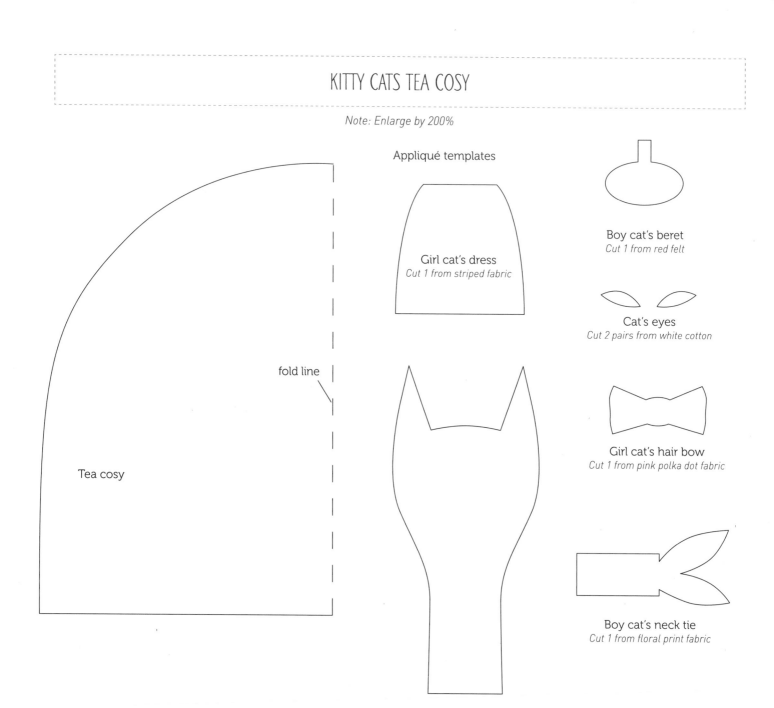

Appliqué templates

Girl cat's dress
Cut 1 from striped fabric

Boy cat's beret
Cut 1 from red felt

Cat's eyes
Cut 2 pairs from white cotton

Girl cat's hair bow
Cut 1 from pink polka dot fabric

Boy cat's neck tie
Cut 1 from floral print fabric

fold line

Tea cosy

Body
Cut 1 from grey felt and 1 from apricot felt

INDEX

PUBLISHER'S ACKNOWLEDGEMENTS

This book would not have been possible without the input of all our fantastic crafty contributors. We would also like to thank Cheryl Brown, who has done a great job of pulling everything together and Sophie Yamamoto for her design work. Thanks to Kuo Kang Chen for his excellent illustrations, and Vanessa Davies for her photography. And of course, thanks must go to the fantastic team at Mollie Makes for all their help, in particular Lara Watson, Helena Tracey and Katherine Raderecht.

For more information on Mollie Makes please visit molliemakes.com

PAVILION

Whatever the craft, we have the book for you – just head straight to Pavilion's crafty headquarters.

Pavilioncraft.co.uk is the one-stop destination for all our fabulous craft books. Sign up for our regular newsletters and follow us on social media to receive updates on new books, competitions and interviews with our bestselling authors.

We look forward to meeting you!

www.pavilioncraft.co.uk

First published in the United Kingdom in 2014 by
Pavilion Books Company Limited
1 Gower Street
London
WC1E 6HD

Copyright © Pavilion Books 2014

ISBN 978-1-90939-729-3

A CIP catalogue record for this book is available from the British Library.

10 9 8 7 6 5 4 3 2 1

Reproduction by Mission, Hong Kong
Printed and bound by CT Printing Ltd, China

This book can be ordered direct from the publisher at www.pavilionbooks.com

Photography by Vanessa Davies
Illustrations by Kuo Kang Chen